D1525617

ISLAM RECONSIDERED

Islam Reconsidered

*A Brief Historical Background to the Religion
and Thought of the Moslem World*

Kenneth Oster

An Exposition-University Book

Exposition Press   *Hicksville, New York*

Contents

Introduction

WE ARE ABLE to identify with the oil embargo, sky-
jacking, plane-burning, assassinations, and hostages. They have
touched our lives. They bring the word "Arab" to our minds. We
activate the dormant recesses of our otherwise active memories
and are able to add to that indistinct concept something about
"a thousand and one nights" and Allah-worshiping, camel-driving
desert riders. Somewhere in the hazy background something
about the court jester, the royal harem, and, of course, the Arabian
horse helps to compound the confusion. We are aware of a
Crusade-hating, corsair-spirited, sultan-dominated society that
venerated the caliph, bowed toward Mecca, and lived on dates
and goats' milk. The Arab? Well, he's the one they call a "Muslim," and Arabia, his desert home that "grows" oil. Correct?
Rather, yet lamentably incomplete!

Numerous factors have contributed to our general ignorance
of the Arab and our apathy toward his religion, culture, and
contributions to the West. Prime among these is the fact that we
have fallen heir to the seventh-century anti-Muslim attitudes that
burst forth from pen and mouth under the severe pressure of
defeat and humiliation, as the "sword of Islam" inexorably swept
through formerly Christian provinces of the Middle East. Western
historians and theologians, with but few exceptions, have filled
libraries with a bias that inhibits the average reader from any
other viewpoint. Few have ever taken the time or trouble to look
at the other side of the coin; though no thinking person can
deny that another side exists. On the other hand, when one is
forced to turn off the air conditioner in his luxury limousine,
turn down the thermostat in his sprawling ranch house, and

7

forgo swimming in his no-longer-heated pool, coming to the shocking reality that there is a third world with which he must contend, there begins to develop a certain coercion to untangle his confused ideas. It begins to touch his very life and affect his personal comfort.

Is it not time to reconsider the Arab? And in doing so, to try to understand Islam, his religion, the spark that motivates his conscience and energizes his decisions? This task, we believe is long overdue—the burden of the chapters that follow.

In all fairness to Islam, however, we must first take a critical look at ourselves as Christians—Christians as compared to Christ, Christianity as exemplified by its proponents, and Christianity as it set the world stage on which Islam was to play such an important role thirteen centuries ago when Mohammed became the "Prophet of Islam." Any self-appraisal runs the risk of too intimate involvement. It will also be easy to allow prejudices and preconceived ideas to blind us to a fair reconsideration of Islam. To avoid these two possibilities, we shall endeavor to catch a cosmic glimpse of both Christianity and Islam. By that we mean a disentanglement in the issues. We will endeavor to take up a position in outer space, and view the events and forces at work on Mother Earth as relates to the Middle East.

ISLAM RECONSIDERED

I
Heritage of
Abraham the Hanif

ABRAHAM WAS a man intimately connected with God's plan for saving the lost. The Noachian flood exterminated the wicked antedeluvian world, and in only one short chapter, chapter eleven of Genesis, is recorded the genealogy of the three sons of Noah to the tenth generation, which was that of Abraham. Ten generations are passed by with no comment whatsoever, but almost all the rest of the book of Genesis, to the end of the fiftieth chapter, is a detailed account of the life of this one man and his immediate descendants; of his walk with God and God's communion with him; of his pure faith in one Creator God and God's promises to him—all of which won for Abraham, the father of the faithful, the title of *Hanif*, the pure monotheist.

> Say: Lo! As for me, my Lord hath guided me unto a straight path, a right religion, the community of Abraham, the upright (Hanif), who was no idolater (37. 6:162).

> And (O Muhammad) set thy purpose resolutely for religion, as a man by nature upright (Hanif), and be not of those who ascribe partners (to God) (37. 10:106).

So much the more amazing and admirable was Abraham's faith in One God, when contrasted to the rampant polytheism of his contemporaries, which persisted relentlessly for centuries to come.

Abraham "believed in the Lord; and he counted it to him for righteousness" (Gen. 15:6). Twenty-four centuries later, Mohammed, using the editorial *we,* speaks on behalf of God:

11

"Verily, we chose him in the world, and lo! in the Hereafter he is among the righteous" (37. 2:130). Nevertheless, the Lord, in an unbelievable demonstration of condescension assured the Patriarch, that the world's Redeemer would come through his seed (Gen. 15:9-17). When Abraham was eighty-five, his wife Sarah had still not borne him a son, so he married Hagar, her Egyptian servant-girl, from whom was born Ishmael, Abraham's firstborn! Upon him the venerable old man lavished his love, wealth, and attention. Ishmael was his son, and he would be his heir, for, thought Abraham, has not "God heard" my prayer (Ishmael)? But this human fabrication was not of God's devising. At the age of fifteen, Ishmael fell heir not to his father's estate, but to a half-brother who would be given the coveted birthright. About five or six years later when Isaac passed the ceremony of weaning (Gen. 21:8), Ishmael, being quite a young man, felt keenly the chagrin of his status and the impact of ostracism. He with his mother was "cast out" (Gen. 21:10) of Abraham's household.

It is impossible to feel the full impact of the tremendous emotions that plagued Abraham. "The thing was very grievous in Abraham's sight because of his son" (Gen. 21:11). Much less can we appreciate the struggle that raged in the hearts of Hagar and her innocent son, Ishmael! Two generations later Joseph was cruelly sent away from his father's house, but at least he had the assurance that his father had not turned against him; rather, he was the victim of the hatred of his wicked half-brothers. Ishmael, on the other hand, was "cast out" by his own father—a godly man who had trained him in the way of the Lord. Before the birth of Isaac the Lord had made a pertinent statement about Abraham, and on it depended the divulgence of a secret regarding the destruction of the cities of the valley. The Lord's reasoning was put thus:

> And the Lord said, "Shall I hide from Abraham that thing which I do, seeing that Abraham shall surely become a great and mighty nation, and all the nations of the earth shall be blessed in him? For I know him, that he will command his children and his household after him, and they shall keep the way of the Lord,

to do justice and judgment; that the Lord may bring upon Abraham that which he hath spoken of him" (Gen. 18:17-19).

We emphasize that the time this was spoken, the only son Abraham had was Ishmael. Not only did Ishmael learn to keep the commands of the Lord, but he, along with the descendants of Isaac and, for that matter, Abraham's entire household would "do justice and judgment." Having lived almost one score years under the personal tutelage of his own beloved and loving father, Ishmael witnessed the faithfulness of Abraham and learned the principles of righteousness that were imparted to him.

Abraham was known by all in that country for his faith in the One God:

> God called Abraham to be a teacher of His word, He chose him to be the father of a great nation, because He saw that Abraham would instruct his children and his household in the principles of God's law. And that which gave power to Abraham's teaching was the influence of his own life. . . .
>
> Abraham's influence extended beyond his own household. Wherever he pitched his tent, he set up beside it the altar for sacrifice and worship. When the tent was removed, the altar remained: and many a roving Canaanite, whose knowledge of God had been gained from the life of Abraham, His servant, tarried at that altar to offer sacrifice to Jehovah (46. 187).

It is possible that Ishmael as a teenager was not far away when Christ and the two angels were hosted at the door of his father's tent (Gen. 18:1-15; John 8:56). It is not impossible that Abraham's heir apparent was permitted to see the divine visitor on the ominous occasion when his wife "laughed" at the very thought of having a son in her old age!

But in time the announcement was fulfilled and Ishmael had to be cast out. The transgression of the second commandment carried a curse with it that would be felt by the children to the third and fourth generation, but the victims of those who broke the seventh command were ostracised to the tenth generation (Deut. 23:2). A parallel ostracism was that of Jephthah, whose half-brothers determined they would never allow their illegitimate half-brother to receive any of their inheritance—until they found themselves in trouble and needed his pugilistic qualities to deliver them from their enemies (Judg. 11:2 ff).

Ishmael seems to have been ostracised and disinherited as a bastard not only for ten generations, but for eternity. Today, thirty-seven centuries later, we find that the enmity and hatred between the house of Isaac and the house of Ishmael has not abated one iota, but becomes inflamed at the slightest provocation. The solution to the Arab-Israeli conflict seems to be beyond the ken of human devising. Undoubtedly it will not be solved until the Prince of Peace returns with healing in His wings.

We return briefly to Isaac and his twin sons, Jacob and Esau. The latter, Isaac's firstborn, closed the gap between the Arabs and Jews (though not called by those terms at that time) somewhat by marrying Bashemath, the daughter of Ishmael, sister of the twelve sons of Ishmael (Gen. 36:3). From this union sprang Reuel (same name as the father-in-law of Moses, also called Jethro [Gen. 36:10; 2:18]).

Jacob, the supplanter or deceiver, changed to Israel at his conversion at the Brook Jabok, had twelve sons also and one daughter (Dinah). The birthright was to be passed on through the line of Judah, his fourth-born son by Leah. Thence, through the house of the future king David the promised Messiah was to come.

The apostasy of idol-worship took the descendants of David into the seventy years' Babylonian Captivity. Upon their return, the Children of Promise went to the other extreme of legalism. "When the fulness of the time was come, God sent forth his Son, made of a woman, made under the law, that we might receive the adoption of sons" (Gal. 4:4, 5). Here we find a third family becoming intimately involved in the plan of salvation—those of the Gentile world who become heirs of the promises made to Abraham through adoption (Gal. 3:29). This is to be accomplished by faith in the grace of God (Eph. 2:8).

Consider now the three families: The Arabs, as lineal

descendants of Ishmael, Abraham's firstborn, by social standards should be the natural heirs to the heritage of the patriarch Abraham. The torch of truth that was lit by the pure monotheist Abraham was handed to Ishmael.

In early times the father was the ruler and priest of his own family, and he exercised authority over his children, even after they had families of their own. His descendants were taught to look up to him as their head, in both religious and secular matters. This patriarchal system of government Abraham endeavored to perpetuate, as it tended to preserve the knowledge of God. It was necessary to bind the members of the household together, in order to build up a barrier against the idolatry that had become so widespread and so deep-seated. Abraham sought, by every means in his power, to guard the inmates of his encampment against mingling with the heathen and witnessing their idolatrous practices; for he knew that familiarity with evil would insensibly corrupt the principles. The greatest care was exercised to shut out every form of false religion, and to impress the mind with the majesty and glory of the living God as the true object of worship (48. 141).

The Lord said to Abraham, "And as for Ishmael, I have heard thee [verily God had heard—and called his name "God shall hear"—Ishmael]: Behold, I have blessed him, and will make him fruitful, and will multiply him, exceedingly; twelve princes shall he beget, and I will make him a great nation" (Gen. 17:20).

When the bitter moment of separation came, God promised;

"Let it not be grievous in thy sight because of the lad, and because of thy bondwoman; in all that Sarah hath said unto thee, hearken unto her voice; for in Isaac shall thy seed be called. And also of the son of the bondwoman will I make a nation, because he is thy seed." And Abraham rose up early in the morning, and took bread, and a bottle of water, and gave it unto Hagar, putting it on her shoulder, and the child, and sent her away; and she departed and wandered in the wilderness of Beersheba. And the water was spent in the bottle, and she cast the child under one of the shrubs. And she went, and sat her down over against him a good way off, as it were a bowshot; for she said, "Let me not see the death of the child." And she sat over against him and lift up her voice, and wept. And God heard the voice of the lad; and the angel of God called to Hagar out of heaven, and said unto her, "What aileth thee, Hagar? fear not; for God hath heard the voice of the lad where he is. Arise, lift up the lad, and hold him in thine hand for I will make him a great nation." And God opened her eyes, and she saw a well of water; and she went, and filled the bottle with water, and gave the lad drink. And God was with the lad; and he grew, and dwelt in the wilderness, and became an archer. And he dwelt in the wilderness of Paran: and his mother took him a wife out of the land of Egypt (Gen. 21:12-21).

Despite all these advantages, the Arab world has been cut off from the "Children of Promise." Even in later New Testament times the Apostle Paul, uses the two wives of Abraham as an allegory (Gal. 4:22-26) depicting the ostracism of the children of Ishmael.

Then come the Children of Israel, given the glorious promises of temporal as well as spiritual prosperity and blessing on condition of obedience. They failed, and lost the promised birthright and the honored place among God's people. Then the third family, the Gentile world comes along, and we who had neither blood connection nor spiritual claim—through the grace of God fall heir to *all* the promises made to Abraham! Wonder of wonders, amazing grace! But do we really, as wild olive branches grafted onto the olive tree "contrary to nature" deserve the birthright? Only "if thou continue in his goodness: otherwise thou also shalt be cut off" (Rom. 11:22). And let us make no mistake, to continue in "his goodness" we must by all means recognize the possibility of the "natural branches" (Rom. 11:21) being grafted on again to the mother tree from which they have been lopped off. As Gentiles saved by grace, we owe a debt to the Jews and Arabs that cannot be lightly passed off. God has a place for them. With love and sympathetic understanding, we owe to these desert children of Abraham all that God has freely granted us. By our own standards, we are constrained to admit that they are even more worthy as "natural branches" than we who at best are "wild branches"!

II
Pre-Islamic
Middle East

The Prophetic-Historic Perspective

DURING THE thirteen centuries of their coexistence, often with sabers rattling and at sword point, Muslims and Christians have cast blame on any and all except the real culprit. In Revelation 12:7 we read of a war in heaven! A cosmic view opens before us. Christ and Satan are personally involved. The field of battle is transferred from heaven to earth (Rev. 12:8, 9). Immediately "the inhabiters of the earth" become participants, "for the devil is come down unto you, having great wrath" (Rev. 12:12). Man's infidelity, rebellion, and consequent destruction have been the studied aim of Satan. To accomplish this, he, "the god of this world hath blinded the minds of them that believe not, lest the glorious gospel of Christ, who is the image of God, should shine unto them" (2 Cor. 4:4). His satanic majesty has stirred up the thinking of the children of God, aroused every hateful and sinful passion in the breast of the unwary, engendered misapprehension and hatred in the emotions of one of God's creatures against his fellowmen, and gloated over the war and bloodshed that has resulted.

All this was as Satan would have it. This was what for ages he had been working to secure. His policy is deception from first to last, and his steadfast purpose is to bring woe and wretchedness upon men, to deface and defile the workmanship of God, to mar the divine purposes of benevolence and love, and thus cause grief in heaven. Then by his deceptive arts he blinds the minds of men, and leads them to throw back the blame of his work upon God, as if all this misery were the result of the Creator's plan (47. 284, 285).

17

With this situation in mind, let us stand back and try to get a cosmic perspective of the forces at work. Why should a man be at variance against his father, a daughter against her mother, a daughter-in-law against her mother-in-law? Why should a man's foes be of his own household?

When I was a boy, my friends and I used to delight in taking two puppies from the same litter—two puppies that were growing up together, that played together, ate together, slept together, yes, lived together all the time in perfect harmony. We would take these two puppies and ruffle them up, getting them angry; before long they were fighting each other, and we would stand back and laugh.

With the passing of years I came to see that the clashes of man are but the stirring up of animosity by Satan who stands back and laughs when he gets two men, both claiming to be believers, to hating, fighting, and killing each other. Multiply this fighting and hating and killing between two individuals, multiply that damnable spirit on a national, yes, even an international, scale and you involve the entire world in global conflict.

If we could only refuse to be pawns in the devil's game of death! If we could only have vision powerful enough to recognize that Satan has interposed his evil design on God's eternal plan for our lives, we could avoid most of the tragedies that plague us so frequently and so inescapably.

Fortunately, there is more to be seen than the work of devils. From the cosmic perspective, we are able to draw ourselves out of the involvement, stand back, and view the forces that are at work; we see from this perspective that God works behind and above the scenes of human perception.

When the patriarch Job was afflicted by Satan, he despaired of even life itself, not realizing that God had established limits beyond which Satan could not pass. Satan might take everything from Job except his life.

You will remember the story of the faithful young man Joseph, who was cast into the pit by his brothers, then sold into a life of slavery, and finally cast into an Egyptian prison, all in face of absolute innocence. It was almost impossible for him to understand God's ways. It was only after he was in a position to save the lives of his father and brothers that he came to realize that God was supreme. True, Satan had interposed his evil design and had brought untold anguish to Joseph. But God is most great (*Allahu Akbar,* as the Muslim would say). He would not permit Satan to go beyond a certain limit.

God has set the boundaries of the mighty oceans as an illustration of the limitations of man. To the roaring tide He says, "Hitherto shalt thou come, but no further, and here shall thy proud waves be stayed" (Job 38:11).

We must learn to develop an even greater confidence and certainty regarding the sovereignty of God in all the intricate relationships of mankind. Nations have succeeded one another in majestic review down through the course of human history. Men have held the scepter of power only to pass it on to another, perhaps less worthy than they. Many have boasted of holding the destiny of the world in their own hand, only to be laid low by a Greater Power.

One such was a proud and mighty king who ruled in Babylon. His pride was deflated by a warning message God sent him through a special messenger:

> This matter is by the decree of the watchers, and the demand by the word of the holy ones. To the intent that the living may know that the Most High ruleth in the kingdom of man and giveth it to whomsoever He will and setteth up over it the basest of men. (Dan. 4:17).

If we could only disentangle ourselves from the stranglehold that Satan has thrown around us and get a cosmic perspective of events, we would be reassured to find out that we need not be molested and shoved around by Satan. Rather, we would see the guiding hand of God. If we could only draw aside the curtain, we would behold "behind, above, and through all the play and counterplay of human interests and power and passions, the agencies of the all-merciful One silently, patiently, working out the counsels of His own will." (46. 173).

If only we and the Muslims would take a stance somewhat

removed from the immediate conflict and see the real cause of our differences, we would see Satan in his real role. We would place the blame for our misunderstandings on him where it belongs, and, as fellow-believers in One Creator-God, and brothers of one another, we would in humility and contrition ask for forgiveness, and clasp hands in a bond of brotherhood, faith, and trust.

But more for a clearer understanding of the cosmic war. We glance at the prophecy of Daniel who speaks of the demonic power that was to speak "very great things" (Dan. 7:20), make "war with the saints" (Dan. 7:21), "speak great words against the Most High" (Dan. 7:25), and "think to change times and laws." We see that Satan would so stir men and beguile them that even though taking the name of Christ, many would, in fact be doing the work of "antichrist" (1 John 2:18, 22; 4:3; 2 John 7). These deluded souls would actually be the "synagogue of Satan" (Rev. 3:9). The Apostle Paul permits us another glimpse of the cosmic war by exposing "the mystery of iniquity" which was already hard at work even in his day, one "whose coming is after the working of Satan with all power and signs and lying wonders and with all deceivableness of unrighteousness in them that perish" (2 Thess. 2:7-10).

Through the prophetic gift we are favored with another insight into the backstage goings-on of the cosmic war. Satan instigates individuals to be his ministers who are actually

> false apostles, deceitful workers, transforming themselves into the apostles of Christ. And no marvel; for Satan himself is transformed into an angel of light. Therefore it is no great thing if his ministers also be transformed as the ministers of righteousness; whose end shall be according to their works (2 Cor. 11:13-15).

With almost superhuman effort we disentangle ourselves from embroilment in the affairs of this life and remove to a point in outer space and watch the unfolding of events on planet Earth. We have seen the war started in heaven, the transference of the field of battle to earth, and Satan's treacherous deceptions among men. He made them angry with one another and we saw him rejoice over the bloodletting that went on among mankind due to the machinations he instigated. Then "when the fulness of the time was come, God sent forth his Son, made of a woman, made under the law, to redeem them that were under the law" (Gal. 4:4,5). Christ came to set up His spiritual kingdom, the Church, on earth, that through it the world might be brought to a knowledge of Satan's sophistries, God's love, and man's brotherhood—and be saved. Satan did all he could to distort this truth, hide the providence of God, and mislead souls.

For the next six centuries Satan battled against the newly established Church. At first he attacked it through his human agents and tried to destroy it by persecution and extermination (Rev. 2:10; 6:3,4). Failing to exterminate the Church by barbaric cruelty, he changed his tactics to that of flattery and coddling. The Church was elevated into royal favor when Constantine the Great espoused Christianity and lavished his wealth and attention on it. No doubt it was during this period that Satan managed to enter the Church by stealth (Rev. 2:13) and make it his "seat." Those "that hold the doctrine of Balaam" and "the Nicolaitanes" (Rev. 2:14,15) were prominent in the Church, which condition Christ says "I hate" (Rev. 2:15). Commercialism (Rev. 6:5,6) replaced the original spirit of self-sacrificing love, as avaricious leaders bartered it off for the mundane tinsel of popular prestige.

As we continue to view our breathtaking spectacle of the cosmic war and see how Satan actively transformed the pure Apostolic Church into a Jezebel-ruled community of idolatry, adultery, and fornication (Rev. 2:18 ff.), we begin to understand why, when Mohammed appeared in the early seventh century, he disdained to identify with "Christianity," for their spirituality seemed to have hit rock bottom. It was a picture of "Death," with "Hell" following after (Rev. 6:7,8), as John the Revelator described the status of Christianity during the Dark Ages (53. VII:750).

This then, is the situation, as viewed from our cosmic stance: War in heaven with Christ and Satan as the principle participants. The scene of battle is transferred to planet Earth and all its inhabitants become individually involved. When the "fulness of time" arrived, the Creator, Jesus Christ, effected the incarnation, and established His Church. The Church, then, became the object of Satan's fierce attacks. It did not emerge unscathed, but suffered a dire apostasy—to such an extent that Satan managed to plant his seat in the Church and give it the appearance of Death. Spirituality was gone, and the Church exuded a negative influence.

The New Testament Church teachings on the doctrine of the Trinity and the divinity of Christ have not always been coherently presented, and certainly not without controversy and misunderstandings. And it has been in these very areas where Islam has taken vital issue with the Christianity that confronted it.

From the cosmic vantage point of prophecy outlined briefly above, we noticed the part Satan would play in corrupting the early Church. From the historical view, it is not difficult to trace the steps that led to a distortion of the purity originally instilled within the Church that was founded by Jesus Christ. Though it was a gradual infiltration of pagan customs, the leavening effect received great impetus when Constantine opted for Christianity as the state religion. Because of the preferred status given to Christianity at that time, we question the conversion of the pagans and wonder if, in fact, it was not the Church that was transformed or converted by the influx of pagans, whose customs and beliefs were brought in with them (6. 502).

The simple theology of the primitive Christians was gradually corrupted. The pristine monotheism of the Apostolic Church became clouded by metaphysical subtleties, degraded by popular mythology, and confounded with an ever more popular polytheism. The adherents began to frequent the tombs of saints and martyrs in the hope of obtaining, from their powerful intercession, every sort of spiritual, but more especially temporal, benefit. Edward Gibbon states that "the religion of Constantine achieved, in less than a century, the final conquest of the Roman empire; but the victors themselves were insensibly subdued by the arts of their vanquished rivals" (18. 215).

Corruptions and misrepresentations soon became multiplied in regard to the question of the Trinity, Mariolatry, and the divinity of Christ. The Church of the sixth century developed an astoundingly tolerant spirit of adaptation. In A.D. 431, Cyril, Archbishop of Alexandria, in a famous sermon at Ephesus, applied to Mary many of the terms fondly ascribed by the pagans of Ephesus to their "great goddess" Artemis/Diana. The Council of Ephesus in that year, over the protest of Nestorius, sanctioned for Mary the title "Mother of God." Gradually the tenderest features of Astarte, Cybele, Artemis, Diana, and Isis were all synthesized in the worship of Mary! In this century the Church established the Feast of the Assumption of the Virgin into heaven, and assigned it to August 13, the date of ancient festivals of Isis and Artemis. Mary became the patron saint of Constantinople and of the imperial family; her picture was carried at the head of every great procession, and was hung in every church and home in Christendom (11. 745, 746).

As predicted, Satan seemed completely triumphant in paganizing the Church. Superstitious bishops believed in omens and were haunted by fears of the devil, for their concept of God was that of a jealous, vindictive god who favored his devotees without troubling about their morality. After replacing the worship of God with a worship of saints, it was but a step to replacing the healing saints with the gods and heroes of antiquity. Left to itself the human mind fell back wholly into paganism (32. 392).

The idolatry so strongly opposed by Mohammed took shape as a result of the incorporation into the Church of pagan beliefs widely practiced. Appellations of "Queen of the World," "Queen of Heaven" (Jer. 7:18; 8:2), "Queen of all Saints," "Queen of hell and of all evil Spirits," "Mother of God and men," etc., indicate a marked affinity to the Roman god Juno, the consort of Jupiter, or of Hera, the sister and wife of Zeus. Mary, in like manner, came to be looked upon as both the mother and the spouse of Jesus Christ.

The profanation of the Mother of Jesus as "Mother of God" was closely linked to Isis, the *mater dolorosa* of paganism who was supposed to sympathize with mothers in their sorrows and afflictions. In his prayer, Lucius (Apuleius) says:

(Thou) by thy bounty and grace nourishest all the world, and
bearest a great affection to the adversities of the miserable as a
loving mother. . . . Thou art she that puttest away all storms and
dangers from men's life by stretching forth thy right hand. . .
and appeasest the great tempests of fortune. . . .

It is, then, only natural that some students have seen her influence as "mother of sorrows" and "mother of Horus," in whom
the *Greeks saw their grief-stricken Demeter searching for her
daughter Persephone raped by Pluto, on the Christian concept of
Mary.* The motif of mother and child appears in many statuettes
which have been found in her ruined shrines on the Seine, Rhine,
and Danube, and which the early Christians mistook for the
Madonna and Child, and little wonder since it is still difficult to
differentiate between the two types.

The epithet "Mother of God" (Theotokos) as applied to Mary
seems to have been used at first by Alexandrian theologians at
the close of the third century, although it does not appear in any
extant writing of that period. It became common in the fourth,
being used by Eusebius, Athanasius, Gregory of Nazianzus in
Cappadocia and others, Gregory saying that "the man who does
not believe Mary was the *Theotokos* has no part in God (27. 54
[italics supplied]).

Pre-Christian Roman cults emerged in the Church with
"Christian" names. Diana, the virgin goddess contributed something to the worship of the Virgin Mary. The Roman Juno, the
Greek Hera, the Carthaginian Dea Caelestis, the Egyptian Isis,
the Phoenician Astarte, and the Babylonian Mulitta had all been
queens of heaven. (30. 93-95). Egypt had no small part to
play in this prostitution of the simple teachings of Christ. The
extant figurines of Isis nursing Horus are a striking similarity to
familiar representations of the Madonna and Child. (30. 122-
33). Thus it becomes apparent that this heresy of profligate
paganism, that of a male god raping a female deity, from which
abominable, incestuous union was produced a "son of god"
(Matt. 26:54), was conceived in the Canaanite cults of Ras
Shamra and Egypt, incubated in Greco-Roman mythology,
especially the mystery religions, borne full stature in the apostate
Church, and foisted off onto the non-Christian world as truth.

So widespread and general was this concept of the Trinity— a father god, a mother god, and a physical biological offspring to make a third, a son god—that the residents of Mecca in central Arabia had installed in their pantheon a Byzantine icon of the virgin so that the "Christian" merchants on the *via odorifera,* who frequented the entrepôt would also have somewhat to worship along with the other pagan merchants. (35. 4). Well might Mohammed, the son of Abdullah (the slave of God), speaking on behalf of God ask in consternation: "O Jesus, son of Mary! Didst thou say unto mankind: 'Take me and my mother for two gods beside God?' " (37. 5:116).

Certainly Mohammed was not speaking only to his fellow-countrymen, the pagans of Arabia, when he declared his clarion call *La Illaha illa l'Lah* (There is no god but God). His burden was not only to the pagans of Arabia, but equally to the already apostatized and spiritually dead "Christians" of Rome and Byzantium. How close he was to a reemphasis of the commandments given to Moses against idolatry and image worship!

Thou shalt have no other gods before me. Thou shalt not make unto thee any graven image, or any likeness of anything that is in heaven above, or that is in the earth beneath, or that is in the water under the earth: thou shalt not bow down thyself to them, nor serve them: for I the Lord thy God am a jealous God, visiting the iniquity of the fathers upon the children unto the third and fourth generation of them that hate me; and shewing mercy unto thousands of them that love me, and keep my commandments (Ex. 20:3-6).

Franz Cumont looks at the seemingly interminable list of paganisms that were adopted by the Church and claims that Christianity did not stop there. "It took from its opponents their own weapons," he asserts, "and used them; the better elements of paganism were transferred to the new religion" (9. xi, Introduction by Grant Showerman).

John William Draper observes that the inhabitants of Italy and Greece were never really alienated from the idolatries of the old times. "At the best," he writes, "they were only Christianized on the surface. With many other mythological practices, they forced image-worship on the clergy" (10. I:368).

We cannot escape the picture of sixth-century popular Christianity as it was drawn on the canvas of the Middle East. In his *History of Dogma,* Adolph Harnack writes that the Church, under the leadership of Pope Gregory the Great, presented itself as the most intimate union of Christianity of the first order with a subterranean, thoroughly superstitious, and polytheistic "Christianity." He also traces the direct evolution of the heathen temples, rites, and rituals into the accepted norms of the Christian Church. (22. IV:304,305).

A fifth-century Manichaean had become aware of the wretched condition of the Christianity of his time. It was altogether too apparent to be missed. He accused his contemporaries in these words:

> The sacrifices you [the Christians] change into love-feasts, the idols into martyrs, to whom you pray as they do to their idols. You appease the shades of the departed with wine and food. You keep the same holidays as the Gentiles; for example, the calends and the solstices. In your way of living you have made no change. Plainly you are a mere schism; for the only difference from the original is that you meet separately (2. 253).

By assuming a cosmic perspective, we will see how Satan had succeeded in corrupting the simple, soul-saving truths of Christ's legacy. Arnold J. Toynbee beautifully entitles one of his books *Civilization on Trial,* from which I underscore the following:

> As the Muslims saw it, the Prophets of Israel were all right, and Jesus was God's last and greatest prophet before his final messenger Muhammad. *The Muslim's quarrel was not with the Prophet Jesus but with the Christian Church,* which had captivated Rum [the Byzantine, or Eastern "Roman" Empire] by capitulating to pagan Greek polytheism and idolatry. From this shameful betrayal of the revelation of the One True God, Islam had retrieved the pure religion of Abraham. Between the Christian polytheists on the one side and the Hindu polytheists on the

other there again shone the light of monotheism; and in Islam's survival lay the hope of the world (42. 76 [italics supplied]).

Mohammed's quarrel was verily *not* with Christ, as Toynbee declares, but with the type of "Christianity," infested with the worship of idols and the adoration and deification of saints which rankled his very being.

A Muslim writer corroborates this conclusion in positive language. Abdullah Usuf Ali sees very perceptively the steps of degradation taken by the Church. Placing the blame on the "chaos of idolatrous sects," he explains why the inhabitants of Egypt generally welcomed the forces of Islam in A.D. 639 (1. I:412,413).

Harnack summarizes the status of Christianity at the birth of Islam:

> In its external form as a whole this Church is nothing more than a continuation of the history of Greek religion under the alien influences which have affected it. . . . There is no sadder spectacle than this transformation of the Christian religion from a worship of God in spirit and in truth into a worship of God in signs, formulas, and idols. . . . It is the religion of the ancient world tacked on to certain conceptions in the gospel; or, rather, it is the ancient religion with the gospel absorbed into it (23. 236-58).

The testimony of history amply verifies the prophetic picture given of the future of the Early Church. Were it not for the latter, one would be tempted to despair, but included in the prophetic revelation is also the final triumph of the forces of good over the agents of evil. We as "heirs of God, and joint-heirs with Christ" (Rom. 8:17) have the privilege, and the responsibility to look into the causes of estrangement between Christendom and Islam, accept blame for our having misrepresented Christ, and determine to bridge the gap in the last hour of history, finding fellowship with our Muslim brothers as they receive a new vision of Christ, for "neither is there salvation in any other: for there is none other name under heaven given among men, whereby we must be saved" (Acts 4:12).

III

The Muslim World

The Birth of Islam

THE SAD STATE of affairs in the Christian world which
has been described in chapter two was certainly a misrepresentation of Christ. The iconoclastic controversy and the disputes on
the nature of Christ and the Trinity, Mariolatry, mediation of
saints, relics, and prayers for the dead had so split up the Church
by the beginning of the seventh century that North Africa, Egypt,
Palestine, Syria, and the East had all broken away from the
Mother Church, either by excommunication or by their own will.

The virtual polytheism to which the Byzantine Church had
fallen heir made nominal Christianity little better than the pagans
of Arabia during the period known by Arab historians as the
Jahiliyah days, usually rendered "time of ignorance" (25. 87).
It refers to the spiritual condition during the period immediately
preceding Islam in which Arabia had no dispensation, no inspired
prophet, no revealed book; for the cultured and lettered society
as that developed by the South Arabians can hardly be called
"ignorance."

The Bedouin of the Jahiliya age had little if any religion.
Though divinations by means of drawing arrows was practiced
(See Ezek. 21:21), the pagan Arabian developed no mythology,
no involved theology, and no cosmogony comparable to that of
the Babylonians (25. 90). His deity consisted of natural objects
such as trees, wells, caves, and stones. The well in the desert with
its cleansing, healing, life-giving water very early became an
object of worship. Zamzam's holiness, according to Arabian
authors, was pre-Islamic and went back to the time it supplied
water to Hagar and Ishmael (Gen. 21:12-21).

Bedouin deities were myriad. The forbidding desert sun compelled the caravans to travel by night and even the shepherds to graze their flocks by moonlight, hence moon-worship gained the ascendency, in contrast to sun-worship in the more tolerable climates of Canaan and Persia. The urban population of the Hijaz, which became the cradle of Islam, developed a worship of three daughters of Allah: Al-Uzza (Venus, the morning star), al-Lat (from *Ilahah,* "the goddess"), and Manah (from *maniyah,* "allotted," the goddess of fate) (25. 99).

Hubal (from Aramaic for vapor, spirit), evidently the chief deity of the Ka'bah, was represented in human form. The pagan Ka'bah, which housed Hubal and hundreds of other idols, was an unpretentious cubicle (hence the name) of primitive simplicity, serving as a shelter for a black meteorite which was venerated as a fetish. Muslim tradition ascribes credit to Adam for having first built it, and to Abraham and Ishmael for rebuilding it after the Flood. (37. 2:118-21).

Allah (*allah, al-ilah,* the god) was the principal deity of Mecca. Mohammed was the son of Abdullah (the slave of Allah), a member of the Quraysh tribe, a direct, lineal descendant of Abraham through Ishmael, and at that time custodian of the sacred precincts of the revered Ka'bah. Other pagan deities such as *Nasr* (vulture) (37. 71:23), and *Awf* (the great bird) have creature names and suggest totemic origins.

In the face of this almost universal polytheism in Arabia as well as that permeating the Christianity of his day, Mohammed proclaimed fearlessly the belief in One God in his clarion creed *La Ilaha illa l'Lah* (There is no god but God). The urgency of his message cannot be gainsaid. It was long overdue. Monotheism, we must emphasize, is a high mountain that must be scaled, not a valley into which man naturally slithers. "No people have been recorded or discovered with an inborn craving or of race-bias making for monotheism, but on the contrary the lower and prevalent popular instinct is always polytheistic" writes Farnell (13. 85). Two outstanding exceptions of monotheism illuminate the pages of history outside Israel. The first is that of Akhenaten, otherwise known as Amenhotep IV of Egypt. The monotheism

he instituted at Tel-el-Amarna near Thebes is regarded by some
historians as the most remarkable achievement in the history of
religion, for due to the will power of a single man acting in
direct opposition to the wishes and emotions of a powerful priest-
hood, he was able to establish his new religion (13. 85).

It was a royal Pharaoh of profound vision that could carry
through so audacious a revolution; and Professor Breasted rightly
regards him as the first recorded idealist in history, but an idealist
born "out of due time" and out of all sympathy with the religious
bias of his people. Therefore his work prospered only in his lifetime. His monotheism was obliterated immediately after his
death; and in his memory he may be said to have suffered a
posthumous martyrdom, being only remembered as "the criminal
of Akhetaten," his name for the modern Tel-el-Amarna (7. 345).

The second exceptional emergence of a monotheism of an
extraordinary caliber is that of Zarathustra of Iran. If Richard
Frye's recent research is correct, the first year of the Zoroastrian
Era was 588 B.C. (16. 28), making him a contemporary of the
prophet Daniel, who lived past the fall of Babylon in 539 B.C.
and into the first years of the reign of Cyrus II the Great. The
latter instituted Zoroastrianism as the state religion which was
faithfully upheld by Darius I and his successors. The supremacy
of Ahuramazda, who was the only god evoked by the Persian
royalty, was not challenged until Artaxerxes II (404-359 B.C.),
an Achaemenid of another line who was challenged by Cyrus the
Lesser, a descendant of Cyrus the Great (45. 16). Hitherto the
unusual monotheism espoused by Cyrus the Great and his successors for almost a century and a half throws light on the exalted
position and title attributed to that unique personage by Isaiah
the prophet who called him the Messiah, the Lord's "Anointed"
(Isa. 45:1), a title shared only by Jesus, the Lord's "Anointed."

Polytheism, not to mention hedonism that is everywhere, is
natural to man, a product of his own natural instincts, and almost
universally acclaimed outside the Judeo-Christian-Muslim world.
Monotheism, on the other hand, and in contrast, is a revealed
truth, not the outcropping of any man's private cogitations. For

that matter, any light or information one might have on God, His nature or character or attributes must be had by special revelation. Man, of himself is incapable of finding out the Almighty (Job 11:7). The natural man slides into polytheism as has been demonstrated so clearly throughout the history of the world. Polytheism, no doubt with Satan's promptings and insinuations, is the result of man's naturally sinful inclinations. Even a brief glance at the history of polytheism reveals an almost universal bent toward it. Its vast preponderance in both sacred as well as profane literature (outside the Judeo-Christian-Muslim world) is quite apparent. In the light of this revelation, man—be he caliph or Bedouin, king or peasant—has no inherent human greatness whatsoever, and thus no humanism to give rise to vain glories. The only greatness admitted by Islam is the lasting one of sanctity, and this belongs to God.

To summarize, the heritage of Abraham, as the Lord Himself testifies (Gen. 18:1-19), was a pure monotheism unparalleled by any other nation. This faith in One God, sometimes bedimmed, but always there, was passed on from generation to generation through the family of Ishmael, the father of the Arabs until it emerged again in full bloom with Islam.

The Rapid Spread of Islam

This faith in one God was the message, the central theme, and burden of Mohammed's life. For the proclamation of this greatly needed message in a preponderantly polytheistic society, the prophet of Islam staked his all. At a crucial moment the battle lines were drawn up. The small band of about three hundred poorly armed Muslims was greatly outnumbered by the pagan Meccans. Mohammed had spent the night on his knees praying not only for victory but also for the very survival of Islam. He poured out his heart repeatedly: "Lord, fulfill Thy promise. If this handful of Muslims perishes today, there will be no one left to worship Thee" (14. 84).

Under normal circumstances the Battle of Badr in A.D. 624

would have been an insignificant skirmish between two unknown Arab tribes in the desert, but at this one encounter the existence of Islam was at stake. The two-year-old Muslim community was threatened with annihilation by the superior enemy force. The course of world history depended upon the outcome of this battle.

Mohammed, the founder and prophet of Islam, was born fatherless *circa* A.D. 570 and orphaned at an early age. He was nurtured by his grandfather Abdul Mutalib, who died shortly thereafter, then taken to the home of his uncle Abu Talib.

The inherent and acquired godlessness in Arabia disturbed Mohammed. At the age of forty he claimed to have had a vision in which he heard a voice telling him to "recite" God's messages. These "recitations" (Koran) came to be looked upon as sacred instructions from God. The Koran is composed of 114 chapters, or *suras,* of varying lengths, arranged roughly according to length. Noteworthy among many, is the injunction to "overcome evil with good" (37. 13:22).

It is not claimed that the revelations came down in written form, but in a form of inspiration that provided Mohammed with the words to speak to others. As he gave his messages over a period of time, various people wrote them down as they remembered them. A later secretary, Zaid, under the direction of Caliph Othman, collected all existing recensions and portions recorded on potsherds, stones, camel shoulder blades, leather, and memories of men to form one volume—the Koran. It contains Islamic legislation and deals with such items as pilgrimage, marriage, prayer, and many others. New Testament stories as well as Old Testament stories appear in several suras. Apocalyptic and eschatological scenes are vivid in description. Disapproval of frivolity, contempt of arrogance, and encouragement of almsgiving as an atonement for sin reflect Nestorian overtones. Jesus is often spoken of as a messenger.

When Mohammed's preaching began in Mecca in A.D. 610, the Quraysh tribal chiefs immediately recognized in his preaching a threat to their traditional way of life, and they began to oppose him. Later on, two Arab tribes, Aws and Khazraj, in Yathrib, a city about 300 miles north of Mecca, called upon Mohammed to arbitrate their differences. He accepted their invitation, and thus found a new home for Islam. Under heavy persecution of his fellow-Meccans, he executed his "flight" from Mecca in the summer of A.D. 622, which event, referred to by the Muslims as the *hijra,* marks the beginning of the Islamic era. That year became the first year of the Muslim calendar.

Under Mohammed's successful administration Yathrib soon came to be called *Madinat-un-Nabi,* "The City of the Prophet," or *Al Madina,* "The City." Relieved of persecution, Islam grew rapidly in this friendly atmosphere. A humble mosque (Arabic *masjid,* place of worship, passed to English through Old Spanish *mesquita*) was erected with a thatched roof, where the Muslims would gather for their daily devotions.

It was under these settings that the Meccans, incensed that they had allowed Mohammed to escape their grasp in Mecca, determined to annihilate him and his followers in Medina. With cavalry and camel brigade, they marched northward. Mohammed and the three hundred of his faithful devotees, hearing of the imminent attack, prepared for the worst. Battle lines were drawn up at Badr, a village about twenty miles southwest of Medina (25. 116), where the tide turned in their favor.

We must always maintain with steadfast earnestness our confidence in God's overruling providence. God could easily have allowed the meager force of three hundred Muslims to be wiped out by the thousand Meccans who attacked them. Many have considered Islam as a tragedy and a menace. Many have looked upon its advance as a calamity to civilization. Many have wished that God would have forestalled this mighty force when it was still an infant—and He could have—but did not, apparently because it was in His divine providence that Islam should arise and play its role in *Heilsgeschichte.*

Ellen G. White, in commenting on the setting up and pulling down of world emperors, says:

All earthly powers are under the control of the Infinite One. To the mightiest ruler, to the most cruel oppressor, he says, "Hitherto shalt thou come, but no further" (Job 38:11). God's power is constantly exercised to counteract the agencies of evil; he is ever at work among men, not for their destruction, but for their correction and preservation (48. 694).

Not only are events known by God, but in His divine providence, He brings about men and movements to establish His sovereignty and knowledge among the people of the world—and He is no respecter of persons—calling to His cause some whom mortals might, in their pride and arrogance, consider the most unlikely and unworthy!

Within a short time, new Muslim victories brought Khosrow Parviz, the Persian emperor, to his knees, and Muslims occupied the territories of the already fragmented Byzantines.

In Arabia the Battle of Badr was but the harbinger of a greater victory, as Mohammed negotiated in the Pact of Hudaibiyah for a peaceful entry into Mecca, subsequently destroying all idols and making that city his capital. His creed was proclaimed in the clarion call *La Illaha illa l'Lah* (There is no god but God). This cry against the polytheism of the pagans as well as the apostate Christians was to be sounded for centuries to come. Mohammed's quarrel, as we mentioned in the last chapter, was not with Christ, but with "Christianity," not with those who were "surrendered" to God, but to those who perpetuated heresies.

The dogma of the Incarnation became inextricably involved with the conflicts of the metropolitans, rivalries of ecclesiastical potentates, noisy councils, imperial laws, deprivations, exiles, riots, and schisms. Thus the dismembered "Christian" empire was easy prey to the lieutenants of Mohammed (4. 6).

The Church in Syria and Egypt, with embittered feelings toward their European counterparts, who considered them heretical, almost welcomed the benevolent regime of Islam (4:12). Bell claims that "the persecution of Christian by Christian, if less bloody, was if anything, more bitter in spirit than the persecution of Christian by Pagan had formerly been" (4. 5).

By the time of his death in A.D. 632, Mohammed had by the

sheer force of personality and strong religious conviction brought all of Arabia under the banner of Islam. His successor was Abu Bakr, the first of four caliphs to rule the burgeoning state from Medina. At the Yarmuk Gorge in A.D. 636, he utterly defeated the forces of Eastern Roman Emperor Heraclius, who had fought the Persians through Syria and Egypt. This signal victory was rapidly followed by the fall of Damascus and Jerusalem, which meant the total occupation of Syria and Palestine by the Muslims. Islam soon numbered among its adherents multitudes who had been brought up under other faiths. The Persians and the Aramaic and Coptic Christians who adopted Islam soon far outnumbered the Arabs. These all exercised no little influence upon their conquerors (4. 189). It has been asserted that it was these neophytes who brought into Islam the spirit of partisanship and bigotry to which they themselves had been so long accustomed (4. 190).

God's providence can be traced in Islam's conquests of these lands. The Muslims were actually welcomed by major portions of the population who had existed under the iron rule of Rome. The testimony of one such is cited by Butler:

> The statement of Abu l-Faraj (Bar Hevraeus) gives the judgment of a Monophysite of much later date, but probably reflects something of the feelings which prevailed at the time. "When our people complained to Heraclius," he says, "he gave, no answer. Therefore the God of vengeance delivered us out of the hands of Romans by means of the Arabs. Then although our churches were not restored to us since under Arab rule each Christian community retained its actual possessions, still it profited us not a little to be saved from the cruelty of the Romans and their bitter hatred toward us (4. 166).

Victory had whetted the appetite of the Muslims. Alexandria fell in A.D. 639 not because of the chivalry of the invaders, but because of the treachery of Cyrus, the Patriarch! Finding the Monothelite compromise which Heraclius had negotiated unacceptable to the native Egyptian church, Cyrus endeavored to procure its acceptance by force, and his tenure of power was marked by a severe persecution directed against the Copts, which sapped still more their allegiance to the Byzantine Empire, called Roman by the Arabs (4. 165), and paved the way for the entry of the Arab Muslims.

Egypt, one of the most ancient lands, was not to be ruled by native Egyptians! Ezekiel, about the year 587 B.C. had boldly predicted that "it shall be the most lowly of the kingdoms, and never again exalt itself above the nations; and I will make them so small that they will never again rule over the nations" (Ezek. 29:15). Persians, Greeks, Romans, and Byzantine Greeks had held the scepter over the land of the Pharaohs. Holy Writ still declared that "there shall no longer be a prince in the land of Egypt" (Ezek. 30:13). Now Heraclius' prince, Cyrus, the Patriarch, having mistreated the Egyptians, made them ready to turn to the Arabs. In Egypt today thousands of the same Hamitic or Coptic people will be seen, but not one has ruled the country. After the Arab conquest, Turks, French, and British ruled for different periods until today the Arabs are again in full control, fulfilling the words of prophecy and demonstrating further evidence of God's marvelous providence.

The Muslim navy under the spiritual zeal of the third caliph, Othman (A.D. 644-656), subdued Cyprus, brought Carthage under tribute, and attacked Rhodes. The Berbers of North Africa were "converted" and Afghanistan was made a Muslim province. As the coffers of Damascus, Jerusalem, Alexandria, and Ctesiphon successively filled to overflowing the Arabs' treasury, Muslim leadership suffered an equal and opposite decline in spirituality.

The nepotistic Caliph Othman made sure he placed his relatives in important positions. One such was Muawiyeh, who was made governor of Damascus. He founded a dynasty that ruled the Middle East for ninety years with ten caliphs. Muawiyeh seized the caliphate from Ali, the son-in-law of Mohammed, and with his successors launched military expeditions that overthrew, one by one, Cyzicus on the Sea of Marmora, Qayrawan in Tunisia, Algeria, and Morocco along the North African coast, as gems in their growing empire.

When Uqbah, the conqueror of North Africa, reached the

Atlantic he was distressed that he could not go any farther. He is said to have spurred his horse into the sea, raised his hands to heaven and exclaimed: "Almighty God, but for this sea I would have gone into still more remote regions, spreading the glory of Thy name and smiting Thine enemies" (35. 120).

An obscure Berber freedman called Tariq ibn Ziyad tackled one of the most dramatic conquests. Cueta was his jumping-off place—for just a few miles across the Straits was Spain. He took possession of the Rock of Gibraltar, which has ever since borne his name (Jabal Tariq—"Mountain of Tariq") and then with 7,000 men, mostly Berbers, descended upon the province of Algeciras and routed an army of 25,000 under Roderick, the last of the Visigothic kings. Their relentless swords swept on. Cordova fell by a ruse, Malaga surrendered, Elvira was taken by storm, and Toledo was entered undefended remaining the center of culture and learning for three centuries.

In the east, Basra, on the lower Tigris, became the launching site for campaigns into Central Asia. As Muslims made accessions in Uzbekistan, with Bokhara and Samarkand and Tashkent as chief cities, they made contact with Turks who would subsequently play a major role in the Abbasid Caliphate and later take Constantinople which the Caliph Othman had attempted to do three times, but was repulsed by the mysterious "Greek Fire" (25. 201).

Sind, in the lower Indus Valley, was Islamized by A.D. 713. Muslim Pakistan (Land of the Pure) today attests to the permanency of the Muslim conquest in that area.

It was in October, 732, a hundred years since Abu Bakr had announced the death of Mohammed, that the army of Abdur-Rahman ibn Abdullah, governor of Spain, made contact with the Franks under the command of Charles of Heristal, called Martel—"The Hammer." In a wood between Tours and Poitiers, the Arab leader was killed, and his men hurried out of what threatened to be a bitter cold winter battle. Before this turning point, the Arabs had invaded France and progressed halfway to the English Channel. Even later they took Avignon, advanced on Valence and Lyons, spread through Burgundy, and

threatened Paris. Thus Islam had reached its farthest extent in
the West.

Mention was made of the fact that Muawiyeh usurped the
caliphate from Ali, son-in-law of Mohammed, and was duly
elected fourth caliph. The resultant feud caused the supporters
of Ali to revolt against the Omayyads in A.D. 747. The feud
continued indefinitely, until Abu-l Abbas was elected caliph by
acclamation in Kufa. He declared his intention to purge the world
of the hated Omayyad usurpers. On August 5, 750, Marwan the
Second, the last Omayyad caliph, was slaughtered with every
member of his household save one (25. 279-87).

Abbas, the exterminator of the Omayyads, transferred the
capital to Bagdad where his family met a similar fate almost two
hundred years later. Not until then did Islam really begin to
internationalize. Having absorbed the culture of the many nations
it had conquered, Islam, under the Abbasids, established the
capital at Bagdad on the banks of the Tigris. As center of the
Muslim world, Bagdad was distinguished alike by its wealth, its
luxury, its literary brilliance, its schools of learning, and medical
institutions (4. 312).

Harun-ar-Rashid (A.D. 786-809), of Arabian Nights fame, is,
no doubt, the best known caliph of the Abbasids. His reign ushered in the golden age of Islam, an unrivaled era of literary and
scientific advance. Constantinople was soon outdone by Bagdad,
with the port of Basra assuming great maritime importance. By
A.D. 850 Muslim ships had reached China to trade for silk. A
considerable Muslim colony was established in Canton. Trade
was carried down the east coast of Africa as far as Madagascar.
In the Mediterranean, Muslim shipping vied for first place with
that of Venice and Genoa. Enormous quantities of coins minted
in Tashkent and Samarkand from A.D. 700 to 1500 are constantly
showing up around the Baltic states. A gilt-bronze cross found in
an Irish bog bears the inscription *Bismillah* ("In the name of
God") in Arabic characters (29. 28).

Of the superiority in learning and arts of the Muslim East
over Western Europe at this time there can be no question.
Muslim Spain, under Umayyad Abdur Rahman III (A.D. 912-61)

and his rejuvenated dynasty excelled equally—an entire chapter by itself not dealt with in this book. All branches of learning received great impetus. The first *bimaristan* (hospital) in Islam was built in Bagdad after the pattern of Gundishapur in southwest Persia. The Persians Ali al Razi, ibn Sina, and others produced learned works in Arabic. Razi's works on medicine were translated into Latin in Vienna in 1565 and later gained him the reputation of being one of the keenest original thinkers and greatest clinicians not only of Islam but of the Middle Ages (25. 366). Astronomy and mathematics flourished; the *Bait al Hikmeh* (House of Wisdom), in Bagdad, became world famous. Caliph Al Ma'mun's (813-833) astronomers came very close in estimating the exact circumference of the earth by measuring the length of a terrestrial degree (25. 375). Imagine this, when Galileo (1564-1642) nearly seven hundred years later, in 1632, was tried by the Inquisition and forced to abjure belief in the heliocentric theory of the solar system! Copernicus (d. 1543) is regarded as the founder of modern astronomy for having established the theory that the earth rotates daily on its axis. Western genius has blinded Westerners to the credit due the Muslims. Intellectual advancement lost its perspective. It was this kind of religious bigotry that kept Europe so dark in the Middle Ages while the Muslim East reached new heights of intellectual and scientific development. The Jalali Calendar, originated by Omar Khayyam (d. 1123/24), has a much greater degree of accuracy than the more familiar Julian Calendar (reformed by Gregory XIII in 1528).

Science flourished under Harun while his contemporary Charlemagne (742-814), with whom he was on friendly terms, was, with his fellow-monarchs in Europe, dabbling in the elements of writing their names! History books are replete with graphic accounts of those days—seeming stagnation in "Christian" Europe and the fantastic strides in literature, science, art, medicine, astronomy, navigation, mathematics, jurisprudence, and almost every branch of endeavor in the Muslim East. Beyond the intellectual pursuits, tremendous areas were added to their territorial limits. Turkish mercenaries from the steppes of

Central Asia gradually became the masters in the Abbasid Caliphate in Bagdad, and eventually pressed their claims into Asia Minor and became the forerunners of the Ottoman emperors who in time, threatened Vienna and harassed all of Europe from the North Sea to the Iberian Peninsula! Largely unnoticed by Western churchmen was the part the Ottoman Turk played in the great drama of the Protestant Reformation, which subject we will take up in detail in chapter five.

The ebb and flow of armies, the passage of time, and the changing ideologies of men everywhere have contributed to a misunderstanding and lack of appreciation of Islam by Christians. Despite these sociological factors, for thirteen centuries the Muslims have been echoing the clarion call from the summits of a thousand minarets every day: *La Ilaha illa l'Lah* (There is no god but God)! Though many changes have evolved in various aspects of life and religion, the keynote of monotheism as spelled out in the Koran comes through with brilliance, unequivocal and untarnished. It shines full on the majesty, the greatness, the absolute sovereignty of the One Creator God.

> Say, He is God, One
> God, the Eternal.
> He begetteth not nor is begotten
> And there is none equal unto Him (37. 7:52).

Considering the muddied waters, stirred up by the interminable controversies for six centuries following the establishment of the Christian Church, the world was in need of a clear, unambiguous, unequivocal and understandable proclamation of the truth about the unity of God, an echo, if you please, of Abraham. Mohammed's was that voice.

> Islam has perpetuated up to our own day the Biblical world, which Christianity, once Europeanized, could no longer represent; without Islam, Catholicism would quickly have invaded the whole of the Near East, and this would have involved the destruction of Orthodoxy and the other Eastern Churches and the Romanization—and so the Europeanization—of our world up to

the borders of India; the Biblical world would have died. One could say that Islam has had the providential role of halting time—and so of excluding Europe—in the Biblical part of the globe and thus of stabilizing, and at the same time universalizing, the world of Abraham, which was also that of Jesus; Judaism having emigrated and been dispersed, and Christianity having been Romanized, Hellenized and Germanized, God 'repented'— to use the expression from Genesis—of this unilateral development and gave rise to Islam, which He caused to spring forth from the desert, an ambience or background of the original Monotheism (40. 69).

By accepting truth where truth is, and recognizing in Islam a call to the worship of the One Creator God, and in the Muslim a fellow-believer in Him, the mental attitudes are disposed for a dialogue that leads to understanding and acceptance of that spiritual birthright which he has lost through the heritage of Jacob and Christ. Our dialogue becomes no longer a dichotomy of polemics, but one of mutual respect and love; not one of contention and proof, but of enlightenment and acceptance.

IV

Apostasy Contained

AT THE HEART of every pearl is a grain of sand. This grain of sand is foreign, strange, abrasive, painful, destructive. The pearl is nature's way of combating the undesirable element that has intruded the clam shell. The secretion from the body of the clam to "contain" the harmful grain of sand and surround it develops into a costly and beautiful jewel. It is nature's way of combating evil. Nature doesn't just happen. It is the outworking of a divine master plan. The Creator God made provision for any and all so-called emergencies or accidents—for the immediate counteraction and eventual eradication of any element contrary to His divine, eternal, beneficent design.

When a tubercular element begins to develop in one's lung, the entire body goes into immediate defensive action. The chemical and physical properties all work together to surround the tubercular area with a shell of calcium. If given an opportunity, the afflicted area will be completely "contained" within a solid shell of calcified substance, thus entirely closing off the tubercular virus, and preventing its spread and infection to other parts of the body. Were it not for this built-in defense system, the presence of the infection would soon contaminate the entire lung and bring on the loss of the lung, and death to the person. Cooperation with the laws of nature is vital to the preservation of life.

The identical process that we observe in the formation of the pearl and the calcification and containment of tuberculosis in the realm of physical nature can also be traced in the processes of human nature, for the author of both is the all-knowing Creator who made all. The only reason why we are so slow to recognize

42

---

divine providence in the affairs of human relations and the rise and fall of nations is that we become intimately involved with and are a part of the problem ourselves. I urge you again to extricate yourself mentally from the entanglement of daily affairs for a while. Stand back in solemn meditation and catch a cosmic view of the forces at work. You will begin to see the grain of sand or the tubercular virus of satanic passion—foreign to the plan of God, malignant, painful, and damnably destructive. But you will also see nature's counteraction, yes, God's method of "containment" and cure.

Thus far we have traced two very strange aspects of the historical record. The first, the apostasy in the Christian world; the second, the miraculous beginning, growth, and effectiveness of Islam. Through the centuries these two worlds of thought have had a traditional antagonism, one to the other. They have viewed each other as enemies. Protagonists of each have considered themselves as the depositories of truth, and have looked upon any antagonists as those who were inspired by Satan. Taking a cosmic view of the entire situation, however, we find that in the early church when it was pure, during the time when the companions of Jesus were still living and giving guidance, one, Paul by name, made the following remark as he was preaching to the pagan Greeks in Athens. Speaking of the one true Creator-God in contrast to the gods that were made by hand, worshipped by the idolators of Athens, he spoke of Him as the One who hath made of one blood all nations of men:

> And hath made of one blood all nations of men for to dwell on all the face of the earth, and hath determined the times before appointed, and the bounds of their habitation, that they should seek the Lord if haply they might feel after Him and find Him though He be not far from every one of us because He hath appointed a day in the which He will judge the world in righteousness by that man whom He hath ordained (Acts 17:26 ff.).

In this speech, the Apostle Paul pointed out very definitely that nations come and go not because of any prowess of their leader, not because of any military might that they might gather, but because God, in advance, has appointed the times for their

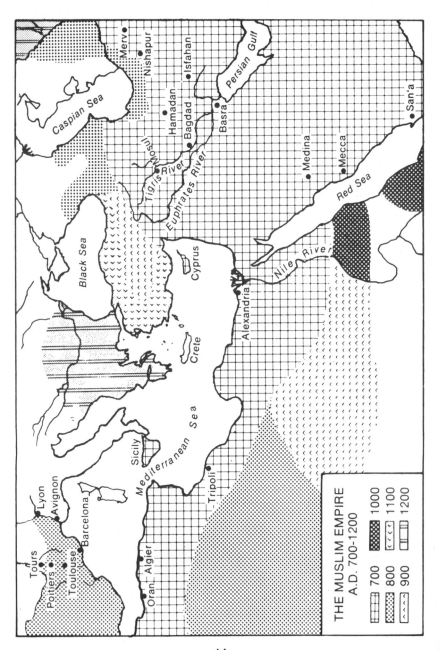

THE MUSLIM EMPIRE
A.D. 700-1200

700 800 900 1000 1100 1200

44

coming and the bounds of their habitation, or the boundaries of the areas which they should possess. And as he continues it is very plain that the purpose of God in allowing these nations to come, to rise, to fall, and to pass off the scene of action was that the people might seek the Lord, that they might repent and recognize Him as the Creator and worship Him. Why? For the hour of His judgment is come.

It is only as we stand back and get a cosmic viewpoint of the great controversy that we understand God's purpose in history. It is only then that we can get an overall view of the great conflict. We can think of Him, God, as moving the nations in order to win certain points along the way. God raises up nations according to His good will and when their time comes He deposes them and puts them out of the way. Once again I refer to the statement in the book of the prophet Daniel, who, speaking to King Nebuchadnezzar, of his day, said: "That the living may know that the most High ruleth in the kingdom of men, and giveth it to whomsoever he will" (Dan. 4:17).

It is as impossible for man to go beyond the bounds or limits that God has set for him as it is for the waves of the mighty ocean to go beyond their shores. To the ancient prophet Job, God likened the advance of man to the waves when He said, "Hitherto shalt thou come but no further, and here shall thy proud waves be stayed" (Job 38:11).

God has never allowed the affairs of man to go out of control. He, in His divine providence, is in absolute control and always has been and forever will be.

From this cosmic stance let us take another look at the contemporary situation in which Islam arose. Within one hundred years of Mohammed's death, in A.D. 632, his followers had not only united and consolidated the warring tribes of the Arabian Peninsula, but had overrun the expansive territories to the east as far as the steppes of Central Asia. They had conquered the Zoroastrian Persians and humiliated the Eastern Roman emperor by slashing at Byzantium's underbelly. The rapid progress across North Africa, the conversion of the Berber tribes, and the crossing into Andalusia came in quick succession.

Only eighteen years after the defeat of the Muslims south of Paris in the Battle of Tours in 732, the center of administration of the vast Muslim forces was to transfer from Damascus to Bagdad. There the golden age of Islam was hailed as a period of enlightenment and progress, of freedom of thought and expansion of every branch of learning. Science and literature, mathematics and philosophy received great impetus under the patronage of benevolent caliphs more interested in *belles lettres* than in war.

The ascetic lifestyle of the early caliphs was replaced by the resplendent luxury of the House of Abbas and prosperity and popularity became the order of the day in Bagdad. Palace guards were recruited from mercenaries from Transoxiana, who forthwith espoused Islam with a vengeance and in time became the masters. Toward the end of the thirteenth century of the Christian era, these rugged neophytes began to spread their influence northward through Asia, among the Tatars in the valley of the Volga, north of the Black Sea and Caspian Sea.

Nikudar Ahmad (reigned 1281-84), the third Ilkhan (who ruled in Iran) was the first of these rulers to accept Islam. (52. XVII:717). It wasn't, however, until the reign of the seventh Ilkhan, Ghazan Mahmud (1295-1304), that Islam was finally recognized as the state religion of the Mongols (51. II:1077). Genghis Khan (c. 1167-1227) described himself as "the scourge of God sent to men as punishment for their sins" (25. 483). He had already, by the first half of the thirteenth century, shaken every kingdom from China to the Adriatic. After his death, and before the birth of Timur, these clans, christened Turks by the men of letters and called Tatars by their neighbors of that day, were nominally Mongols *pro tem*. But like the clans of Scotland they stuck to their family names. They learned to write in different letterings, and a lot of them were converted, to some degree, to Islam, others to Buddhism. They emerged into the pages of history in various countries, and nearly always caused trouble.

Practically the entire eastern frontier of all European states had a common border with the "Golden Horde" (so-named because Jochi had covered his tent with cloth-of-gold), the

Mongols who overran that area. Batu (1226-1255), grandson of Genghis Khan (son of Jochi, eldest son of Genghis), became the Khan of Kipchak in 1227, an area that he extended indefinitely westward from the Aral region into Eastern Europe. At his death, his western frontier ran roughly from the mouth of the Danube in the south, by the Carpathians to Kholm and Lublin, and thence northeastward to the Gulf of Finland and Lake Ladoga (36. 127).

The relations between the Mongols and the Christian nations of Eastern Europe were extremely precarious. Batu Khan had exacted an annual levy from the Christians. At his death, his brother and successor, Bereke Khan, faced a general rebellion on the part of the Christian world. At the command of Pope Alexander IV a general crusade was preached against the Mongols. But though the rage of the Christians was great, they very typically lacked the united energy that might have availed them against their enemies; and while they were yet breathing out denunciations, a Tatar host, led by Nagai and Tulabagha, appeared in Poland. After a rapid and triumphant march the invaders took and destroyed Cracow, and from there advanced as far as Bytham (Beuthen) in Oppeln, from which point they eventually retired, driving before them a crowd of Christian slaves. From this time the Mongols became for a season an important factor in European politics (52. XVII:717).

In 1236 Georgia and Greater Armenia were overrun. Tiflis and Kars both fell. (On the opposite side of the continent, Ogdai had just despatched two armies to Korea and China, south of the Yangtze.) Batu pounded Bulgari, capital city of Bulgaria and crossed the Volga, pushing through the forests of Perga and Tambov until he burst upon the "beautiful city" of Ryazan which fell December 21, 1237. An eyewitness who survived the deluge describes the barbarity:

> The prince, with his mother, wife, sons, the bayars and the inhabitants, without regard to age or sex, were slaughtered with the savage cruelty of Mongol revenge; some were impaled, some

shot at with arrows for sport, others were flayed or had nails or
splinters of wood driven under their nails. Priests were roasted
alive, and nuns and maidens ravished in the churches before their
relatives. No eye remained open to weep for the dead (52.
XVII:713).

The horrors of Ryazan were repeated in Moscow and Kozelsk,
near Kaluga, Kiev "the mother of cities." Thence the Mongols
divided in two divisions; one, under Batu went to Hungary, while
the other, under Baidar and Kaidu marched into Poland. At
Pest, the former launched his attack. Two archbishops, three
bishops, and many of the nobility were among the slain, and the
roads for two days' journey from the field of battle were strewn
with corpses. The king, Bela IV, was pursued to the Adriatic
coast, everything being devastated en route. Meanwhile Batu
captured Pest, and on Christmas Day, 1241, having crossed the
Danube on the ice, took Esztergam by assault. In the north,
Baidar and Kaidu had carried fire and sword into Poland, laying
it waste.

Following the sack of Bagdad in February, 1258, by Hulagu
(founder of the Ilkhan Dynasty that ruled in Iran from A.D. 1256
to 1335), they stormed and sacked Aleppo; Damascus surrendered in 1260, and while planning to attack Jerusalem,
Hulagu suddenly decided to return to Mongolia.

One hundred years later, under the command of the renegade
Toktamish, of the White Horde or Eastern Kipchaks, the Mongols again marched into Russia. Toktamish, in 1378 seized the
throne of his own Horde as well as of the Golden Horde. He
marched into Russia, captured Serpukhov and Moscow on August
23, 1382. The inhabitants were butchered and the city plundered
and burned. Then he advanced and repeated his atrocities in
Vladimir, Zvenigorod, Mozhaisk, Kimitrov, Pereslaul, and
Kalamna.

The religious affiliation of the Mongols has been questioned.
Though Shamanistic to begin with, in time they adopted Islam
with a vengeance. The "neophyte soon became more Catholic
than the pope"—the Mongols more Islamic than the Arabs.
From the beginning of the fourteenth century (half a century after

the destruction of Bagdad and their liquidation of the Abbasid Caliphate) they nurtured closer relations with Egypt. Embassies passed between the two peoples, and so important was the alliance with the Mongols deemed by Sultan Nasir, ruler of Egypt, that he sent to demand in marriage a princess of the house of Genghis Khan. In October, 1319, the princess landed in Alexandria in regal state.

Timur's (Tamerlane, d. 1405) religious sincerity may be an open question, nevertheless his favoritism of Muslims is well established. When he arrived at Azak on his homeward march in 1390, the natives of the entrepôt pleaded in vain for the preservation of their city. His answer was a command to the Muslims to separate themselves from the Venetians, Genoese, Catalan and Basque merchants, whom he put to the sword, and then gave the city to the flames.

Just before the end of the fourteenth century (1390) Timur brought a temporary setback to the ambitious Bayezid I (1389-1402) of the Ottoman Turks called the "Thunderbolt," but strangely, turned northward to Russia and Turkistan. Meanwhile the Turks, having crossed the Bosphorus, encircled Byzantium, reached the Danube in Bulgaria (July, 1393) and the borders of Albania and Thessaly. At a time when the Hungarian ruler was determined to impose the Catholic faith on its Orthodox population, the Ottomans granted unlimited freedom of religion within the framework of their imperial policies. Sigismund asked Pope Boniface IX for help. To meet this threat, the pope launched another crusade against the Turks. The crusade assembled at Buda and marched down the Danube, treating the Orthodox population as the enemy. At Nicopolis the Catholic army of Sigismund met Bayezid's crack Janniseries. The crusade was a complete failure. Bayezid destroyed the army and ravaged Nicopolis, then advanced to Vidin and Silistria which suffered the same fate, and opened the way into Hungary (41. 47-49).

Rather than pursuing, Bayezid was compelled to return—for another threat awaited him; Timur was knocking on his door. The Battle of Ankara (1402) was a disaster to the erstwhile conqueror. Bayezid's victorious army was defeated and the proud sultan placed in a cage to be the laughing stock of his subjects! His men had refused to fight their fellow-Muslims in Timur's forces. Twelve years before Timur had threatened to do the same thing, but providence seemed to dictate otherwise. If Sigismund's folly had been delayed until after Bayezid's encounter with Timur, or if the latter had pressed his attack in 1390 when all signs indicated a propitious outcome for the great khan, what might have been the future of Europe?

But the conquest continued. Within only a decade of Bayezid's capture (he committed suicide while in capitivity in 1403), his empire was completely restored and ready for the offensive under his younger son, Mohammed I (1413-21). A Hungarian hero in the person of John Hunyadi led another crusade called by Pope Eugenius, defeating the Turks at Belgrade (1441), and advancing to Serbia and Sofia in 1443. A ten-year truce was signed, but the perfidious pope broke the truce and resumed hostilities, this time being firmly outmaneuvered at the Battle of Varna on November 10, 1444. Four years later, Hunyadi suffered another signal defeat at the Second Battle of Kosovo.

The accession of Mohammed II Fethi (Conqueror) in 1451 marked the final stages for the thousand-year eastern metropolis. On May 29, 1453, the ramparts of Constantinople were stormed amid the shouts of "Better Islam than the pope" (41. 60). Mohammed exempted the Christian "clergy from taxes, allowed the church full autonomy in its administration, and permitted religious services to be freely celebrated. . . . This toleration, so far ahead of current practice in Western Christendom, was not youthful romanticism but enlightened statesmanship" (41. 60).

The military exploits of the Mongolian Muslims in cooperation with and under the suzerainty of the Ottoman Muslims following the recouping of the latter under Mohammed the Conqueror provide ample evidence of the correctness of our proposition with regard to the containment of apostasy within Europe. As the conquest of the Balkans continued, Mohammed didn't overlook his interests north of the Black Sea. Crimea was the "pot of peace" that brought the two great Muslim powers together after their confrontation a generation earlier over the "bone of contention," Anatolia, on the opposite coast of the Black Sea. The Genoese merchants who hitherto had monopolized the trade on the Black Sea provided the alibi that Mohammed needed to send an expedition into the Crimea to punish the presumptuous traders. Not only were the Genoese peremptorily driven off, but the principal cities of the Crimea—Kaffa, Sydak, Balaklava, and Inkerman—were brought under the authority of the Sublime Porte. Without delay Mengli Girai, the deposed khan, known locally as the Krim Khan, was restored to the throne, and virtually turned the khanate into a dependency of Constantinople.

The ambivalent puppet played both sides with ill-disguised treachery. Hoping to strengthen his own position, he played into the intrigues of the grand-prince Ivan of Russia. One result was that the Mongols were enabled, and encouraged, to indulge their predatory habits at the expense of the enemies of Russia, and in this way, both Lithuania and Poland suffered terribly from their incursions. The walls of the crescent were deeply being intrenched all the way to the North Sea. Of course, the Mongols could not be expected to confine their raids to the "enemies of Russia." On pretext of a quarrel with reference to the succession to the Kazan throne, Mohammed Girai Khan in 1521 marched an army northward until, after having devastated the country, massacring the people, and desecrating the churches on his route, he arrived at the heights of Varobiev overlooking Moscow. The terror of the unfortunate inhabitants at the sight once again of the dreaded Mongols was extreme; but the horrors which had accompanied similar past visitations were happily averted by a treaty by which the grand prince Basil undertook to pay a perpetual tribute to the Krim Khan. This, however, proved but a truce. It was impossible that an aggressive state like Russia should live in friendship with a marauding power like that of the Krim Tatars. The primary cause of the contention was the khanate of Kazan, which was recovered by the Mongols and lost again to Russia with that of Astrakhan in 1555. The sultan, however, declined to accept this condition of things as final, and instigated Devlet Girai, the Krim Khan, to attempt their recovery.

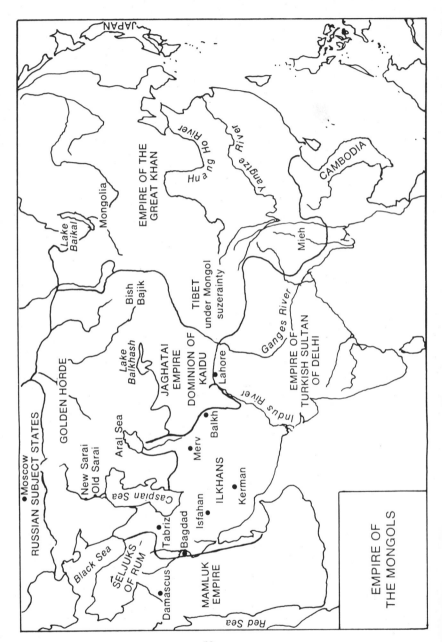

EMPIRE OF
THE MONGOLS

JAPAN

EMPIRE OF THE
GREAT KHAN

Mongolia

Lake
Baikal

Hu a ng Ho River

Yangtze River

CAMBODIA

Mieh

Bish
Bajik

TIBET
under Mongol
suzerainty

Ganges River

GOLDEN HORDE

Lake
Balkhash

JAGHATAI
EMPIRE

DOMINION OF
KAIDU

Lahore

EMPIRE OF
TURKISH SULTAN
OF DELHI

Indus River

Aral Sea

Balkh

•Moscow

RUSSIAN SUBJECT STATES

New Sarai
Old Sarai

•Merv

ILKHANS

Kerman

Caspian Sea

Isfahan

Tabriz

Bagdad

Black Sea

SELJUKS
OF RUM

Damascus

MAMLUK
EMPIRE

Red Sea

52

With this objective the latter marched an army northward, where, finding the road to Moscow unprotected, he pushed on in the direction of that ill-starred city. On arriving before its walls he found a large Russian force occupying the suburbs. With these, however, he was saved from encounter, for just as his foremost men approached the town a fire broke out, which, in consequence of the high wind blowing at the time, spread with frightful rapidity, and in the span of six hours destroyed all the churches, palaces, and houses, with the exception of the Kremlin, within a compass of thirty miles. Thousands of the inhabitants perished in the flames. "The river and ditches about Moscow," says Horsey, "were stopped and filled with the multitudes of people, laden with gold, silver, jewels, chains, ear-rings and treasures. So many thousands were burned and drowned that the river could not be cleared for twelve months afterward" (52. XVII:718, 719). Satisfied with the destruction he had indirectly caused, and unwilling to attack the Kremlin, the khan withdrew to the Crimea, ravaging the countryside as he went.

Eastern Europe was coterminous with the Mongol Muslims. The Balkan Peninsula was under Ottoman control, yea, the Turks were knocking on the very gates of Vienna! The entire eastern and southern coasts of the Mediterranean Sea was a solid bastion of Muslim power, the sea itself under the *firman* of the corsair Khairuddin Barbarosa. The Iberian Peninsula, until the reconquest in midfifteenth century flourished in the arts and sciences, under the enlightened patronage of Umayyad Caliph Abdur Rahman III and his illustrious compatriots. All that remained for the complete encirclement of Europe was the still formidable Atlantic Ocean and the frozen North Sea. The Roman apostasy was thus completely "contained." Nature, when given a chance, will completely "contain" deadly tuberculosis within a shell of calcium within an affected lung, as has already been pointed out. Providence had a way also of containing apostasy within this crescent.

The play and counterplay of world politics whether under the guise of religion or otherwise, whether acted by Arab, Berber, Tatar, Mongol, or Turk, brings us face to face with a most

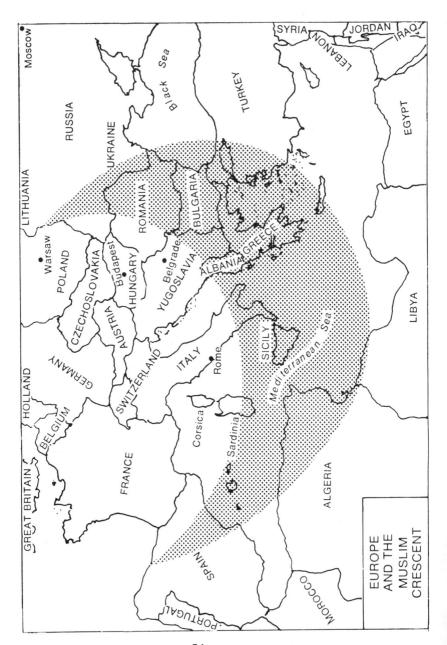

EUROPE
AND THE
MUSLIM
CRESCENT

Moscow

LITHUANIA

RUSSIA

UKRAINE

Black Sea

TURKEY

SYRIA

LEBANON

JORDAN

IRAQ

EGYPT

LIBYA

ALGERIA

MOROCCO

SPAIN

PORTUGAL

FRANCE

GREAT BRITAIN

HOLLAND

BELGIUM

GERMANY

SWITZERLAND

AUSTRIA

CZECHOSLOVAKIA

POLAND

Warsaw

Budapest

HUNGARY

YUGOSLAVIA

Belgrade

ROMANIA

BULGARIA

ALBANIA

GREECE

ITALY

Rome

SICILY

Corsica

Sardinia

Mediterranean Sea

54

unusual situation to which we have referred before. The establishment of frontiers and the movements of peoples and nations are all under the direct control, yea, the prearranged determination of God. The Apostle Paul declared on Mars Hill: He "hath made of one blood all nations of men for to dwell on all the face of the earth, and hath determined the times before appointed, and the bounds of their habitation" (Acts 17:26).
Ellen G. White writes:

> Nothing can happen in any part of the universe without the knowledge of Him who is omnipresent. Not a single event of human life is unknown to our Maker. While Satan is constantly devising evil, the Lord our God overrules all, so that it will not harm His obedient, trusting children. The same power that controls the boisterous waves of the ocean can hold in check all the power of rebellion and of crime. God says to one as to the other, "Thus far shalt thou go, and no farther" (49. July 14, 1881).

We find calm assurance in the affairs of nations when studied and understood in the light of this statement that reflects again that cosmic perspective:

> All earthly powers are under the control of the Infinite One. To the mightiest ruler, to the most cruel oppressor, he says, "Hitherto shalt thou come, but no further." God's power is constantly exercised to counteract the agencies of evil; he is ever at work among men, *not for their destruction, but for their correction and preservation* (48. 694 [emphasis supplied]).

We recapitulate briefly in order to bring together the facts of history thus far presented. We pointed out the gradual and steady apostasy that Satan was determined to bring about in the Christian Church. In order to counteract this Satanic influence, God ordained another power—multilingual, multiracial yet under one banner—that of Islam, to put a barrier around the center of apostasy, by conquering one country after another surrounding Europe. We look at a map of Europe and see how a great protective crescent had inexorably been cast around the enemy of the Reformation. Once Protestantism was established, the wall

began crumbling in places, and the Word of Truth began to
emanate to the far corners of the world in the various missionary
movements.

The Muslim quarrel was not with Christ, but with the "Christianity" which had captured the Roman Empire, given over,
largely, to pagan Greek polytheism and idolatry. From this
betrayal of the revelation of the One God, Islam endeavored to
retrieve the pure religion of Abraham. As the apostasy deepened,
the protective wall that contained it thickened and lengthened.
The Roman hierarchy had so dominated thought and life in
Europe that men had become slaves to the injunctions of the
papal see. The crusades and most military actions in Europe
during the Middle Ages were actions attempting to break through
the crescent. The crescent, albeit unconscious of its cosmic role,
nevertheless did prevent the papacy from enforcing its dogmas
on the rest of the world.

V

The Providence
of God

EXCEPT FOR the very interesting and highly legendary accounts of Harun Ar-Rashid (A.D. 786 to 809) and the fabulous tales of a *Thousand and One Nights,* the West knows very little about the golden age of Islam. With the shifting of the political center of gravity from Damascus to Bagdad came a remarkable amalgamation of Islamic thought with Persian culture and influence. Constantinople was soon rivaled by Bagdad. The call of the prophet of Islam to "seek knowledge even unto distant China" awakened a love of knowledge among the nomadic Arabs such as was hitherto unknown to the world. Such memorable words uttered by the prophet as "the ink of the scholar is more holy than the blood of the martyr," and "he who leaves his home in search of knowledge walks into the path of God," had a salutary effect upon his followers and led to the growth of intense educational activity throughout the length and breadth of the vast Islamic domain. Because of this quest for learning and their indomitable desire to retain the wisdom of the past, universities were founded in Bagdad, Salerno, Cairo, and Cordova.

After the downfall of the Roman Empire, chaos and intellectual stagnation held sway over the apostate Christian nations of Europe. The masterpieces of Greek philosophy, science, and art lay buried under the dark vaults of the monastery and might have disappeared altogether from the world but for the Arab revival and patronage of ancient learning. The Arabs were admirably suited to act the part of mediators and to influence the nations from the Euphrates to Guadalquivir and mid-Africa.

Their unexampled intellectual activity marks a distinct epoch in the history of the world. This fertile, imaginative spirit qualified Islam to play a major role in the preservation of the Bible and the development of the biblical studies of Hebrew and Greek, as they emerged from the golden age of Islam. We will see how in the providence of God these contributed to the development of Protestantism in Germany.

The religio-political storms of the centuries and the various powers that ruled—all had their bearing on the preservation of the Bible, the Muslim powers perhaps more than we realize. For that matter, Islam can be credited for the preservation of a good deal of what is in history. Among the long list of contributions made by Muslims (Persian and Spanish as well as Arab) are contributions in the fields of geography, commerce, art, painting, architecture, literature, philosophy, theology, law, science, medicine, music, astronomy, mathematics, and so on. A detailed account of these would fill many volumes. We are here primarily interested in the preservation and transmission of the text of the Holy Scriptures.

What has rendered the golden age of Islam especially illustrious in world annals is the fact that it witnessed the most momentous intellectual awakening in the history of Islam and one of the most significant in the whole history of thought and culture. The awakening was due in a large part to foreign influences, partly Indo-Persian and Syrian but mainly Hellenic, and was marked by translations into Arabic from Persian, Sanskrit, Syriac, and Greek. Starting with very little science, philosophy, or literature of his own, the Arabian Muslim, who brought with him from the desert a keen sense of intellectual curiosity, a voracious appetite for learning, and many latent faculties, soon became, as we have learned before, the beneficiary and heir of the older, more cultured peoples whom he conquered or encountered.

As in Syria, the Arab adopted the already existing Aramaic civilization, itself influenced by the later Greek. In three-quarters of a century after the establishment of Bagdad the Arabic-reading world was in possession of the chief philosophical works of Aristotle, of the leading Neo-Platonic commentators, and of most of the medical writings of Galen, as well as of Persian and Indian scientific works. In only a few decades Arab scholars assimilated what had taken the Greeks centuries to develop. In absorbing the main features of both Hellenic and Persian cultures, Islam, to be sure, lost most of its own original character, which breathed the spirit of the desert and bore the stamp of Arabian nationalism, but it thereby took an important place in the medieval cultural unit which linked southern Europe with the Near East. Hitti points out that this culture was fed by a single stream, a stream with sources in ancient Egypt, Babylonia, Phoenicia, and Judea, all flowing to Greece and now returning to the East in the form of Hellenism. We shall later see how this same stream was rediverted into Europe by the Arabs in Spain and Sicily, whence it helped create the Renaissance of Europe. (25. 306 ff.).

Hellenistic Influences

At the time of the Arab conquest of the Fertile Crescent the intellectual legacy of Greece was unquestionably the most precious treasure at hand. Hellenism consequently became the most vital of all foreign influences in Arab life. Edessa (al-Ruha'), the principal center of Christian Syrians; Harran, the headquarters of the heathen Syrians who in and after the ninth century claimed to be Sabians; Antioch, one of the many ancient Greek colonies; Alexandria, the meetingplace of Occidental and Oriental philosophy; and the numerous cloisters of Syria and Mesopotamia, where not only ecclesiastical but scientific and philosophic studies were cultivated, all served as centers radiating Hellenistic stimuli. The various raids into "the land of the Romans," particularly under Harun, resulted in the introduction, among other objects of booty, of Greek manuscripts, chiefly from Amorium and Ancyra (Ankara). Al-Ma'mun is credited with the dispatch of emissaries as far as Constantinople, to the emperor Leo the Armenian, himself, in quest of Greek works. Even Al-Mansur is said to have received in response to his request from the Byzantine emperor a number of books, including Euclid.

But the Arabians knew no Greek and had at first to depend upon translations made by their subjects, Jewish, heathen, and more particularly Nestorian Christians. These Syrian Nestorians, who translated first into Syriac and then from Syriac into Arabic, thus became the strongest link between Hellenism and Islam and consequently the earliest Oriental purveyors of Greek culture to the world at large. Before Hellenism could find access to the Arab mind it had to pass through a Syriac version.

Hunayn ibn Ishaq (Joannitius, 809-73) was reputedly the greatest of the famous translators of these Greek manuscripts. His compatriots, ibn-al-'Ibri and al-Qifti, called him a "source of science and a mine of virtue" (25. 313), and by Leclerc "la plus grande figure du IXe siecle," and even "une des plus belles intelligences et un des plus beaux caracteres que l'on rencontre dans l'histoire" (31. I:139).

Stalemate in Europe

While this proclivity for intense study was progressing in the Muslim world, Europe seemed to be suffering an equal and opposite dearth, especially of Greek thought and science. For while in the East al-Rashid and al-Ma'mun were delving into Greek and Persian philosophy their contemporaries in the West, Charlemagne and his lords, were dabbling in the art of writing their names. Not only was this dearth to be seen in learning in general, but more particularly in religious studies. As Latin, the language of the Church, waned and was removed farther and farther from the vernacular, the Bible became less and less known.

As the power of the clergy increased over the illiterate populace, the clergy's interpretation of the Scripture, and theirs only, was permitted. In the apostasy that ensued, which we have outlined in brief sketch, it was noticed that it was the studied plan of Satan to hide the sacred page from the eyes of the people lest his deceptions be exposed. The people of God have always been directed to the Scriptures as their safeguard against the influence of false teachers and the delusive power of spirits of darkness. Satan employs every possible device to prevent men from obtaining a knowledge of the Bible, for its plain utterances reveal his deceptions.

The war against the truth grew in intensity through the centuries, and finally culminated in the horrors of the French Revolution a thousand years later. One perceptive writer remarks:

> The war against the Bible, carried forward for so many centuries in France, culminated in the scenes of the Revolution. That terrible outbreaking was but the legitimate result of Rome's suppression of the Scriptures. It presented the most striking illustration which the world has ever witnessed, of the working out of the papal policy—an illustration of the results to which for more than a thousand years the teaching of the Roman Church had been tending (47. 265, 266).

Under the *Index of Prohibited Books,* as revised and published by order of His Holiness Pope Pius XI, we find this declaration:

> Can. 1385. 1. Without previous ecclesiastical censorship the following works may not be published even by laymen:
> 1) Editions of Holy Scripture, or notes, or commentaries on the same. . . .

> Can. 1391. Versions of Holy Scripture may not lawfully be published in the vernacular, unless approved by the Holy See, or published under the supervision of the bishops and with notes taken particularly from the works of the Fathers of the Church and of learned Catholic writers. . . .

> Can. 1398. 1. The condemnation of a book entails the prohibition, without especial permission, either to publish, to read, to keep, to sell, to translate it, or in any way to pass it on to others. . . .

> Can. 1399.   The prohibition of the following works is implicitly contained in the general law of prohibition:
> 1) Editions of the original text or of ancient Catholic versions of Holy Scripture, even those of the Eastern Church, emanating from any non-Catholic source; translations of Holy Scripture into any language, made, or published by non-Catholics are likewise prohibited (44. xiv, xv, xvii).

Through the centuries this has been the policy of the Roman Church. The results of this policy can be understood only as we view the conditions of the people living under that restraint. The papal power sought to hide from the people the Word of Truth, and set before them false witnesses to contradict its testimony. The Bible was proscribed by religious and secular authority; its testimony was perverted, and every effort made that men and demons could invent to turn the minds of the people from it; those who dared proclaim its sacred truths were hunted, betrayed, tortured, buried in dungeon cells, martyred for their faith, or compelled to flee to mountain fastnesses or to dens and caves of the earth (47. 267 ff.).

The ostensible reason for locking up the truth of God in an unknown tongue sounded logical, but thinking men and women began to see through the perfidy and were willing to give up life itself in order to place in the hands of the common people the words of life in the vernacular once again. Under a profession of reverence for the Bible, Rome's policy was to keep it locked up in an unknown tongue, and hidden away from the people. Yet the Bible continued to bear its testimony throughout the period of papal supremacy (538-1798). In the darkest times there were faithful men who loved not their lives unto death, but kept God's word and were jealous of God's honor.

It was when faithful men in Europe began to let the people know what the Bible really said that the Church took strong action against them. Wycliff, Huss, Jerome were merely the forerunners of a large host of others who were martyred for their determination to unshackle the people from the bonds of Roman slavery. The defendants of this policy explain their cause thus:

What many, indeed, fail to appreciate, and what, moreover, non-Catholics consider a grave abuse—as they put it—of the Roman Curia is the action of the Church in hindering the printing and circulation of Holy Writ in the vernacular. Fundamentally, however, this accusation is based on calumny. During the first twelve centuries Christians were highly familiar with the text of Holy Scripture, as is evident from the homilies of the Fathers and the sermons of the mediaeval preachers; nor did the ecclesiastical authorities ever intervene to prevent this. It was only in consequence of heretical abuses, introduced particularly by the Waldenses, the Albigenses, the followers of Wyclif, and by Protestants broadly speaking (who with sacrilegious mutilations of Scripture and arbitrary interpretations vainly sought to justify themselves in the eyes of the people, twisting the text of the Bible to support erroneous doctrines condemned by the whole history of the Church) that the Pontiffs and the Councils were obliged on more than one occasion to control and sometimes even forbid the use of the Bible in the vernacular. . . .

Those who would put the Scriptures indiscriminately into the hands of the people are the believers always in private interpretation—a fallacy both absurd in itself and pregnant with disastrous consequences. These counterfeit champions of the inspired book hold the Bible to be the sole source of Divine Revelation and cover with abuse and trite sarcasm the Catholic and Roman Church (44: ix-xi).

Interestingly enough, most of the principal Bible manuscripts, used as a basis for our Bible translations, were preserved for posterity in the lands of the Crescent, and were spared the isolationist influences of the Latins of Rome.

Hebrew Scholarship

The study of Hebrew and Old Testament research has as thrilling an affinity with the Arabs as does the study of Greek and the New Testament. Hebrew was a dead language. Scholars did not know how to pronounce the words. They could only look at the characters but they didn't know the vowels that went with the characters, because Hebrew was written like Aramaic with just consonants and no vowels. The Arabs, whose language is a cognate to Hebrew and Aramaic, and which also ordinarily does not insert vowels in the script, began a series of grammatical studies in Arabic. Among the scholars were several Jews who were working on the compendium, on the building up of the grammar of the language and its vocabulary. When they finished, these Jews thought they should have the same thing in Hebrew, that they should try to organize the language and put it together. So they used the same grammatical basis that they had learned from the Arabic, the languages being similar, and recovered the pronunciation of the Hebrew on the basis of the grammatical structures. Guillaume expresses this conviction:

> We owe a great debt to Arabic in the field of Old Testament studies. As soon as Arabic became an imperial language the Jews perceived its close affinity with Hebrew. In the third century of the Hijra the Jews had imitated the Arabs, or rather, the non-Arab Muslims, and submitted their language to grammatical analysis. The grammar of Rabbi David Qimhi (d. ca. 1235), which exercised a profound influence on the subsequent study of Hebrew among Christians, borrows a great deal from Arabic sources. His exegesis, which was founded on his Grammar, is frequently to be traced in the Authorized Version of the Old Testament scriptures (21. ix).

Pronunciation of Semitic languages is based on the form of the word and where it appears and how it is related to the root. So they were able to recover the pronunciation of Hebrew on the basis of analogy. Hebrew, and consequently the Bible, was written one letter after the other. The words were not separated. There were no spaces nor was there any punctuation. The text was just a long series of letters strung out without interruption. When a scholar wanted to work with Hebrew manuscripts, unless he had a pre-Christian Greek Septuagint translation to tell him what it meant, he was unable to get very far. But with the kind of dictionary that was prepared by the Arabic-speaking Jewish scholars, it was possible to recover the Hebrew on the strength of the Hebrew itself. This of course gave a strong impetus to Hebrew scholarship. It resulted in the production of the Masoretic text of the Old Testament as early as the eighth and ninth centuries A.D. The printing of the Hebrew text and the development of the field of Old Testament studies finally developed from this research.

All this illustrates a divine plan in the course of history by which God safeguarded truth and assured a final reformation of the Church. Without Hebrew and Greek, the Bible, its translation into several vernaculars, the preservation of manuscripts and the principles of research, and the liberal spirit of the Arab world, there could never have been much by way of a Reformation.

"The Baptized Sultan"

Thus the stage was set for the wonderful work of the Protestant Reformation. A pertinent actor on this stage was Frederick II (A.D. 1215-50), dubbed the baptized Sultan of Sicily. A descendant of the rugged Normans who invaded and took over the island in 1091 after it had been under Muslim domination for 130 years, Frederick fostered a very progressive and enlightened policy. Under his rule, Sicily became a fertile center for the spread of Arabic science. Among the population Greek, Arabic, and Latin were in constant use as vernacular dialects, but some scholars, particularly Jews, also knew the literary form of these languages. The kings, from Roger I to Frederick II, Manfred, and Charles I of Anjou, drew learned men to Palermo regardless of language or religion. Here, as in Toledo, a troop of learned translators began to make Latin versions from Greek and Arabic. These translations mainly dealt with astronomy and mathematics (33. 348).

Ernest Barker, in his article "The Crusades," elucidates on the continual interchange carried on with the Arabs. He explains that the day-to-day contact with Islam in the East brought familiarity; the toleration, which familiarity can breed, weakened the old opposition of faith and unfaith, just as the Crusades had weakened the distinction between secular and clerical within the bounds of the faith. Not all men in the thirteenth century were of the temper of Frederick II, who used a Saracen army against the pope, corresponded with Arabic scholars, and negotiated with Muslim rulers even when Jerusalem itself was in question. But at any rate scholars showed themselves ready to borrow from Arabic philosophers; some began to study Arabic; and a new spirit of comprehension arose (3. 70,71).

H. A. R. Gibb emphasizes the importance of the link that was Sicily in the transmission of scientific and religious thought to Europe (17. 191). An interesting and pertinent chain of events takes place in connection with this most unusual emperor, Frederick II. He was of the House of Hohenstaufen, king of Germany, and after A.D. 1220 became the emperor of the Holy Roman Empire. In 1225 he married Isabelle of Brienne, the heiress of the king of Jerusalem, and so also became the king of Jerusalem, making him the highest civil authority in Christendom. He retained his court at Sicily, in which he adopted the customs of the Middle East and imbibed the learning and culture of the Arab universities. Obviously, there was a constant play of concurrent forces, and though we cannot measure the exact and separate extent of the main direction in which it was going, we may be assured that Islam acted more profoundly on Western Christendom from its bases in Spain and Sicily than it did from its bases in Mosul and Bagdad and Cairo.

One result of this rich heritage was the founding of the University of Naples by Frederick II in 1224, which was the first institution of higher learning to be established in Europe by a definite charter (25. 612). His almost modern spirit of investigation, experimentation, and research, which characterized his court, marks the beginning of the Italian Renaissance.

Due in part to his "Muslim" connections, the pope considered Frederick an enemy and excommunicated him in A.D. 1227. In retaliation he threatened to invade the Vatican City, which threat, however, never materialized. After being nicknamed "the baptized sultan," the title of "anti-Christ" was also directed against him. The papacy won the struggle with the Hohenstaufens, but more important than that, it also alienated the German people from the Roman papacy and bred lasting suspicion of the Latins, which bore fruit in the Protestant Reformation.

Following the reign of Frederick II, many German princes had the ambition to build universities of their own, following the pattern and example set by their worthy Arabophile predecessor and the Arab caliphs. Thus great impetus was given to the idea of independent thought and explains partially why Germany became the focal point of the Reformation.

The papacy resisted and opposed German Protestantism vigorously, as, on the other hand, German nationalism and opposition to Rome grew in direct proportion. Into this milieu Luther and his teachings came to fruition. Though the emperor, Charles V, in alliance with the pope, secured edicts against Luther at Augsburg and Worms, their efforts came to nought because their armies had to be diverted to meet the new threat of the Muslim Turks.

Ottoman Imperialism and Protestantism

God's cosmic time-clock knows neither haste nor delay. The "Morning Star of the Reformation" had already risen and proclaimed the dawn of a new day. Now it was time for a German, brought up in the tradition of Frederick II, to take the lead in exposing the fallacy of the Roman Church and to issue a call for primitive godliness and belief in salvation by faith in the atoning grace of Jesus Christ. The broad base from which Islam had operated around Europe had proved effective. By the beginning of the sixteenth century, as Portuguese and Spanish seamen had finally circumnavigated the western tentacle of the Crescent, and Dutchmen from the northern ports had put out to explore the world—that is, since the effectiveness of the "containment" principle was finally being negated—again the Muslim power played an active role in providing another kind of protection to the infant life of Protestantism—this time right in the very heart of Europe! We mention but a few high points of great relevance in Turko-Roman relations as they pertain to the rise, consolidation, and spread of Lutheranism.

By 1456 the Mazarin Bible was completed in Mainz, Germany. It is considered to be the earliest book printed from movable type and attributed to Gutenberg. With this, the stage was set for a wide dissemination of the Word of God. Laymen could read and decide their religious convictions for themselves.

In 1478, the year the infamous Spanish Inquisition was instituted by Ferdinand and Isabella, John Hunyadi stopped the Turks under Mohammed II at Belgrade, after which the latter turned his attention for a time to the work of internal consolidation of the Ottoman state.

Martin Luther was born in 1483. Other names of note that enter the picture as contemporaries are Henry VIII of England and Thomas Cromwell. Maximilian, head of the House of Hapsburgs and the Holy Roman Empire (elected to the latter in 1486), aimed at being king of Hungary and arrest the advance of the Ottoman Turks toward the Hapsburg possessions.

The year that Bartholomew Diaz, a Portuguese, discovered the Cape of Good Hope and opened up the searoute to India was 1488. In the same year Ulrich von Hutton was born, destined to be one of the most outspoken critics of the papacy.

Ignatius Loyola (1491-1556), founder of the Jesuits who became the chief instrument of the Catholic Counter-Reformation, was born only the year before Columbus discovered America in 1492, when also hundreds of thousands of Jews were expelled from "Christian" Spain and given asylum by the Ottomans in Turkey.

Vasco da Gama, Savonarola, and Leonardo da Vinci among others appeared just before the turn of the century and played major roles in the European picture.

In 1506, as the first stone was laid for St. Peter's Church in Rome, Maximilian turned to the Diets for help against the "enemy of faith" (15. 9). Ten years later (1516) Charles V became king of Spain and the Netherlands. He was to be a key actor against the German princes. Selim I (1512-20), his opposite number in the Ottoman Empire, along with his successors, in a continuous series of moves and counter moves made it impossible for Charles to exterminate the Protestants. The following year (1517) Luther nailed his ninety-five theses to the church door at Wittenberg, and events rapidly led to the climax. In 1519 Charles inherited the throne of the Holy Roman Empire and within three years Suleiman I the Magnificent (1520-66) mounted his offensive against Central Europe.

About the time that Luther burned the papal bull and earned the wrath of the emperor, Pope Leo X excommunicated him (1520). The greater problem, however, that worried the Central Powers was the fall of Belgrade on August 29, 1521, to the Turks, which opened their road to Hungary.

The new pope, Adrian VI (1522-23), inherited insoluble problems. In the year of his accession, Rhodes, the last outpost of militant Christendom in the Eastern Mediterranean fell to the Turks, and he appealed to Francis I of France, Henry VIII of England, and Charles V to save the island. His appeals fell on deaf ears, and his pontificate went to Clement VII (1523-34), whose efforts at reform were inconclusive, ending in the sack of Rome and his imprisonment in the castle of Saint Angelo.

The future leaders of political Protestantism were making their voices heard. Men like the elector of Saxony and the landgrave of Hesse, as well as the leaders of the free cities of Nurnberg, Ulm, Strassbourg, and Augsburg—already showed strong tendencies toward the Lutheran position.

The year before the Diet of Speyers, a strange rift in European affairs caused Francis I, "Eldest Son of the Church," to appeal to Suleiman to attack the Holy Roman Emperor and the head of the House of Hapsburg, Charles V. Then came the Diet of Speyers (1526) when the papists were unable to enforce the Edict of Worms. That was an auspicious year. On August 29, two days after the defeat at Speyers in religious matters, the Hungarians suffered a fatal defeat at the Battle of Mohacs. The emperor favored his brother Ferdinand as king of Hungary, while Suleiman placed John Zapolya on the throne. After several months the former decided to settle the issue by force, and soundly defeated Zapolya in 1527. In the meantime, the German princes were organizing their forces and understanding more fully the principles of the Protestant Reformation. At this juncture Luther declared, "To fight the Turks is to resist the judgment of God upon men's sins" (43. 135). In fact, the German princes did not wish to support any action that could lead to Zapolya's destruction; Ferdinand's rival might prove useful to the Protestant cause, they mused (15. 30).

The following year, 1529, Suleiman, irate at the defeat of his puppet, invaded Germany and laid seige to Vienna on September 28. Torrential rains hampered his movements. On October 14 he raised the siege and ordered a retreat. This turned out to be the beginning of the end of Turkish military supremacy in Europe, but they still had a lot of firing power for many years to come.

The Lutheran princes, on the other hand, had built up their resources to where they valiantly protested the requirements of Rome and forever secured for themselves the title of "Protestants" (in the second Diet of Speyers, April 19, 1529). They determined to maintain the principle of "no aid without concessions" (15. 36). The concessions Ferdinand was forced to grant them were due to the pressure of the Turks on the eastern frontier. Their protest was a solemn witness against religious intolerance and an assertion of the right of men to worship God according to the dictates of their own conscience (47. 204).

We find a strange reversal of Luther's attitude toward the Turks when Suleiman's army was pounding on the gates of his own (Luther's) fatherland. Whereas earlier, when the Turks were still rather remote, he considered them as God's punishment on sinners, but now he declared, "I fight until death against the Turks and the God of the Turks" (43. 136). It is unfortunate that most Christians have almost entirely adopted Luther's later attitude in regard to their relationships and work among Muslims, not realizing that Luther's later statement was based more on political exigency, rather than on a proper biblical hermeneutics.

Though, to all appearances, Protestantism had already been pretty well established by 1529, Protestants were still faced with threatening possibilities. In 1530, Charles, with the support of Ferdinand and the Catholics, pronounced a death sentence on Protestants at the Diet of Augsburg. With peace reestablished in Western Europe, a solution to the religious question appeared possible. But the Protestants won a reprieve, primarily because of another powerful Ottoman offensive against Hungary and the Empire. In the meantime the Schmalkaldian League had been formed which served Protestantism during this crucial period of its development. On May 6, 1532, with rumors rife that the vast

Ottoman forces had left Constantinople, Charles V made a counter-offer to the League demands for *de facto* recognition: to license limited preaching of Lutheran doctrines outside existing Protestant areas, and to rescind the corresponding powers of the *Kammergericht,* its Catholic counterpart.

The events and decisions of the period dating from the withdrawal of the Turks from Vienna in 1529 to their return in 1532 were highly significant for German Protestantism. They were all conditioned to a large extent by the conflict between Hapsburgs and Turks in Hungary and by fear of Ottoman action against the Empire itself. Stavrianos pertinently observes that "it is paradoxical that an invading Moslem army should have contributed so much to the cause of Protestantism" in its crucial formative stage (41. 78).

"The failure of Charles to act decisively against the Protestants during the years 1530 to 1532," claims Grimm, "permitted the Protestant estates to consolidate the churches in their territories. When his next opportunity to intervene came, fifteen years later, the Protestants were so thoroughly established that force could achieve little or nothing" (20. 213,214).

Almost all major concessions wrested from the Hapsburgs after 1526 were connected with Ottoman activities in Eastern and Western Europe, and the all-important Lutheran campaign for legal recognition in Germany exploited the insoluble Hapsburg-Ottoman conflict over Hungary. The Recess of Speyer of 1526, the Religious Peace of Nurnberg, the Compact of Cadan, the Frankfurt Anstand, the Declaration of Regensburg, the Recess of Speyer of 1542, the Treaty of Passau, and the Religious Peace of Augsburg—all milestones in the Protestant struggle for recognition and the course of the German Reformation—were deeply influenced by the ebb and flow of Ottoman aggression (15. 117).

The tumultuous years did not terminate with the death of Luther in 1546. Protestantism waxed and waned with the ebb and flow of the Turkish armies. But the Protestant leaders, despite limitations imposed upon them by theological restrictions and German abhorrence of the "Infidel," relentlessly exploited the opportunities arising from the secular conflict between Hapsburg and Ottoman. Their perseverance in pursuing such a policy accurately reflects the nature and importance of the Turkish impact on the German Reformation. The Turks diverted the attention of the Hapsburgs from German affairs and made them dependent on Protestant cooperation for the realization of their secular ambitions in Europe, particularly Hungary. The consolidation, expansion, and legitimizing of Lutheranism in Germany by 1555 should be attributed to Ottoman imperialism more than to any other single human factor.

A terminal date for our investigations of the Ottoman imperialism during the formative years of Protestantism is found in September 25, 1555, in the Peace of Augsburg, where the decision of the Reichstag was recorded by which Lutheranism was recognized as an official religion in Germany and legal equality was granted to all worshippers of the faith.

Ellen G. White, in a remark regarding the Turks writes in this connection:

> God's providence had held in check the forces that opposed the truth. Charles V was bent on crushing the Reformation, but often as he raised his hand to strike, he had been forced to turn aside the blow. *Again and again the immediate destruction of all* who dared to oppose themselves to Rome *appeared inevitable; but at the critical moment the armies of the Turk appeared on the eastern* frontier, or the king of France, or even the pope himself, jealous of the increasing greatness of the emperor, made war upon him; *and thus, amid the strife and tumult of nations, the Reformation had been left to strengthen and extend* (47. 197 [italics supplied]).

As Protestantism took root and matured, the leaders recognized more and more the advantage they had gained as a result of the Turks. We would not be far off were we to declare that there would have been no Protestantism had there been no Turk!

VI

The Essence
of Islam Today

Roots of Modern Islam

THE LAST GREAT Arab Muslim power was that of the Mamluks who ruled the state from Cairo for almost three centuries. The whole dynasty was an anomaly, for the Mamluk caliphs were neither Egyptian nor Arab. The very word means "possessed," for they were a family of slaves—slaves of various races and nationalities forming a military oligarchy in an alien land (24. 184). Precursor to them was the rugged al-Malik al Nasir al-Sultan Salah-al-Din Yusuf ibn-Ayyub (Saladin) of Crusader fame (1169-93), born of Kurdish parents in the Mesopotamian village of Takrit on the Tigris River in 1138. A descendant of his, Baybars (1260-77), dealt the *coup de grace* that brought an end to the Crusaders' cause, checked forever the advance of the Mongol hordes of Hulagu and Tamerlane, and, having spared Egypt from their devastating onslaught, set the stage for the final illustrious age of the Arab Caliphate.

From 1250 to 1517 the Mamluks dominated one of the most turbulent areas of the world. Uncultured and bloodthirsty though they were, they displayed at the same time a keen appreciation of art and architectural design, evidences of which still adorn Cairo to this day. Tragic indeed was the dark part of the Mamluk dynasty, bequeathed on inefficient and degenerate heirs, most of them uncultured, many of them illiterate and uncouth (24. 191).

The demise of the Mamluks was brought about in the sixteenth century by the Ottoman Turks, who had originated in Mongolia, admixed with Iranian tribes in Central Asia, and

73

pressed into Asia Minor, where in 1071 under the leadership of Alp Arslan (hero-lion) they overwhelmed Emperor Romanus Diogenes at the decisive battle of Manzikert near Lake Van. They established in Asia Minor the Sultanate of Rum (25. 475). These Seljuk Turks were gradually displaced and replaced by their Turkic cousins who in the first year of the fourteenth century established the Ottoman Kingdom. It was inevitable that Orkhan and his son Osman ("Uthman," Ottoman), after whom the empire came to be named, after conquering the Muslim lands, would orient themselves to the west and expand at the expense of Christian nations.

Rivalries between the Turks and the Mamluks of Egypt was settled in a decisive battle near Aleppo on January 24, 1516. The Ottoman victory was complete. Sultan Selim entered the Syrian metropolis in triumph and soon swept through the Levant into Egypt. Early the following year Cairo fell and Mecca and Medina automatically became a part of the Ottoman Empire. The Egyptian preachers who led the Friday public services invoked God's blessings on Selim, the ruler of a new, non-Arab caliphate!

The sultan-caliph on the Bosphorus became the most powerful potentate in Islam, having inherited not only the power of Damascus, Bagdad, and Cairo, but also the prestige of Byzantium. Germane to our study, and specifically the topic of Islam *today,* is the fact that with the setting up of the Turkish power in the west, the domination of the Arab world began (24. 195).

> Throughout the four centuries of Ottoman domination, beginning with the fall of Cairo in 1517, the whole Arab East was in a state of eclipse. Builders of one of the mightiest and most enduring of Moslem states, the Ottoman Turks conquered not only the Arab lands but the whole territory from the Caucasus to the gates of Vienna, dominated the Mediterranean area from their capital, Constantinople, and for centuries were a major factor in the calculations of Western European statesmen (24. 196).

Mention has already been made in chapter five of the part played by Suleiman the Magnificent in harassing Charles V, the avowed enemy of newborn Protestantism. At the crucial moment in history when the Holy Roman Empire was stronger than it had ever been before in spiritual, moral, and military strength under Charles V and Pope Leo X, it should have been able to exterminate heresies. However, in God's divine plan, bold men like Luther and Calvin and others dared to present "heretical" views, as Protestantism began to emerge. At that very time, the Ottoman Empire, under Suleiman the Magnificent was exalted to the height of its magnificence—at a time when he was able and willing to forestall the nefarious attempts of Charles V from his determination to wipe out Protestantism!

Having come to power for such a time as that—to succor the German princes when threatened with annihilation (15:)—the Ottoman Empire started on its downward course immediately. The course was long and tedious. After the unsuccessful attempt to capture Vienna in 1683, the military role played by Turkey was one of defense rather than offense. The empire began a steady decline and a shrinkage that was accelerated by internal decay and corruption in the eighteenth century when the European powers began to cast covetous eyes toward the far-flung possessions of the "sick man"!

First among the Arab lands to be detached from the empire was Algeria. It was occupied by the French in 1830. Tunisia came next (1881). By 1912 France, Spain, and Italy, the three Latin powers of Southern Europe, had become the overlords of the whole North African territories from Morocco to Libya. The remaining block of the Ottoman possessions in Western Asia, the heartland of Islam, technically remained as parts of the Ottoman Empire until the First World War. It was then that Egypt, which had been occupied by the British since 1882, cut the last tie with Constantinople. Sharif Husayn of Mecca, a descendant of the Prophet, took advantage of the same opportunity to break (1916) with his Turkish suzerains. He incited other Arabs to rise with him. When Mustafa Kamal Ataturk abolished the Ottoman Caliphate in 1924, the Sharif added to himself the title "Caliph of the Muslims." (24. 198).

At this juncture King Abdul Aziz bin Saud, the shrewd and energetic head of the ultraconservative and puritanical Wahhabis of the Nejd, drove Husayn from the throne and between 1900 and 1925 carved out of the central desert a kingdom for himself that extended from the Persian Gulf to the Red Sea.

Then came the mandates! The Western powers parceled out the remaining portions of the Turks: Syria and Lebanon (the only area to retain through all these centuries a major Christian population) to France; Palestine, Jordan, and Iraq to Great Britain, with special privileges accorded her in Egypt and the Sudan. Even Iran came under strong Russian and British spheres of influence.

Thus it becomes obvious that these lands which had not enjoyed independence, or at best had not had Arab suzerainty since 1517, were for four hundred years subject to the Sublime Porte, then autocratically and indiscriminately (as it appeared to them) all placed under mandatory suppression of imperialistic European colonial Christian powers!

In the reconstruction that followed the expiration of the mandates and the selfhood of all these lands is to be found the essence of Islam today.

Thinking men—idealists, philosophers, and politicians—rose to the challenge of the occasion and bred a new generation of intellectuals. Classical Arabic, study of Arabic literature, and research in Islamic history made the Arab conscious of his past glory and of the cultural achievements and contributions of its citizens. Hitti suggests that "the backward look suggested a forward look." He continues:

> Political awakening followed intellectual awakening and the urge for a resuscitated reunited Arab society began for the first time to be strongly and widely felt. Political passivity gave way in favour of political activity (24. 202).

Before concluding the historical background to current Islamic thought, one more pertinent factor of major significance must be mentioned, the threat of Zionism and the creation of Israel. The birth of the latter in 1948 was viewed by Arabs everywhere as an intrusive and dangerous state. But that very fact became the rallying point, as much as if not more than any other single factor, in drawing the fragmented Arab component parts of the Ottoman Empire into a common bond of closer ties with each other. This urge of common interest and the rising feeling of nationalism culminated in the Arab League, whose pact was signed in Cairo in 1945 (even before the creation of the state of Israel), which is today the central spokesman for the Arab if not the entire Muslim world.

Islam after the Reconstruction

In the reconstruction of Islamic thought it must be remembered that the very fiber of Islam is woven on a loom, the warp of which is religion and the woof, the state. There is no room in Islam for the Christian concept of separation of church and state. From its very beginning the two were united. The caliph was as much the religious leader as he was the head of state. When a Caliphate Delegation from India saw Mustafa Kamal Ataturk in Ankara in 1924 asking him to assume the Caliphate, he replied: "Let all the Muslim countries become independent and let there be a League of Muslim Nations, which could be the Body leading the Umma. You can call the Head of such an organization Caliph if you like" (28. 10). As independence was attained and unity sought, throughout the Middle East thought leaders circulated their philosophies, and conferences were called to redefine the ideologies of Islam.

Basic to the beliefs of Islam has always been an uncompromising faith in one God. Inamullah Khan, Secretary-General, World Muslim Congress, Karachi, Pakistan, and editor of the *Muslim World,* in a speech at the centennial celebrations of the American University of Beirut in 1967, epitomized this concept thus:

> When we look at the world today we find it to be the scene of a
> great ideological battle between God-centered ideologies and God-

less cults. It is highly necessary for the followers of God-centered ideologies to understand each other and cooperate in the struggle. "O people with Revealed Scriptures! Let us come together on the concept which is common between us that God is the object of Loyalty," says the Holy Qur'ān (28. 1).

Inamullah Khan analyzes Islamic belief by asking, "What is the meaning of Islam?" Then answers that it means "to be in tune with Allah" (28. 2). Being in tune with God is an ideal not only for the head of state and government officials, but for the rank and file as well.

Sheikh Ahmed Zaki Yamani, Minister of Petroleum and Mineral Resources of the Kingdom of Saudi Arabia, with a Master of Laws from Harvard, exemplifies this high standard in the active way in which he interprets Islam. As another guest speaker at the Centennary Conference at the American University of Beirut mentioned above, he declared:

> Looking from within, the Moslems themselves have to carry the burden and share the blame. Centuries before any contact with the West, a reactionary movement took place, and the elaborate dynamic intellectual stream came to an abrupt standstill after closing the doors of Ijtihad (free investigation). The Shari'a became static and confined to the voluminous traditions of the four schools of thought (Hanafi, Shafie, Maliki, and Hanbali) (50. 51).

Jamaluddin Afghani (1839-97), a Persian statesman, is reputedly the first genuine Muslim modernist. He affirmed that there was nothing in the basic principles of Islam that is incompatible with reason and science. He aroused his contemporaries to develop the medieval content of Islam to meet the needs of a modern society (39. 266). Islam today is faced with secularism and materialism as are also Christian nations. If Islam fails to meet the challenge of spiritual reconstruction, claims Fazlur Rahman, "the only alternative left to them will be some form of secularism, and there is little doubt," he adds, "that this solution is tantamount to changing the very nature of Islam" (39. 309).

Muslim Theology

The struggle of Islam today in the throes of reconstructing a viable, living, practical religion in the face of overwhelming secularism and materialism adheres steadfastly to the following five articles of faith as spelled out in the Koran:

FIVE ARTICLES OF FAITH:

> It is not righteousness that ye turn your faces to the East and the West; but righteous is he who believeth in Allah and the Last Day and the Angels and the Scripture and the Prophets (37. 63).

1. GOD. Belief in the existence of God—His unity, His absolute power, and in the other essential attributes of an Eternal and Almighty Being—is the most important part of Islam as a religion. This is expressed in the creed *La ilaha illa l'Lah* (There is no god but God). An adjunct to this is:

> Say, He is God, One
> God, the Eternal.
> He begetteth not nor is begotten,
> And there is none equal to Him. (37. 2:177).

His creatorship is attested to thus:

> Verily your Lord is God who created the heavens and the earth in six days; then He ascended the throne (37. 7:52).

The Koran speaks of God's power, knowledge, will, hearing and sight, word and works. The attributes of God are listed in the traditional ninety-nine names, "Allah" being the hundredth.

Many critics have found differences in the Muslim's concept of God with those of the God of the Bible and have exploited these differences all out of proportion. With the hundred and more attributes ascribed to Him by Muslim tradition, with which Christian thought coincides, there is ample reason for commonality.

The word "Allah," in the Arabic language, refers no less to
the Creator than the Being whom we Anglo-Saxons call "God."
"Allah" was the name of the chief pagan deity of the Meccans
in the Jahiliyah days. That fact makes Him no less the Creator
in Islam than the word "God" in the English language, a deriva-
tive of the common Teutonic word for a person or object of
religious worship as was applied to all superhuman beings of
heathen mythologies before their conversion to Christianity,
which term was taken over without change to apply to the one
Supreme Being, the Creator (51. X:459).

2. LAST DAY. Eschatological teachings in Islam abound
(12.). Other terms that denote "the Last Day" are the "Resurrection" or "Day of standing up" (37. 2:79), "Day of Separation" (37. 77:14), "Day of Reckoning" (37. 40:28), "Day of
Awakening" (37. 30:56), "Day of Judgment" (37. 1:3), "The
Encompassing Day" (37. 11:38), and "The Hour" (37. 8:186).

Lengthy accounts of the Day of Resurrection, and of the signs
preceding it, are given in Muslim dogmatic theology. The time
of the resurrection is a secret to all but God. Even the angel
Gabriel acknowledged his ignorance on this point when Mohammed asked him about it (8. I:i). However, the *Hadith* (tradition)
teaches that the approach of that day may be known from certain
signs which are to precede it. These signs are in two categories,
"the lesser" and "the greater" (26. 539).

The lesser signs (*Isharatu-s-Sa'ah*) are as follows:

(1) The decay of faith among men.
(2) The advancing of the meanest persons to eminent dig-
nity.
(3) A maid-servant shall become the mother of her mis-
tress (or master), by which is probably meant the
increased sensuality of the last days.
(4) Tumults and seditions.
(5) A war with the Greeks or Romans.
(6) Great distress in the world, so that a man, when he
passes by another's grave, shall say, "Would to God I
were in his place!"

(7) The provinces of Iraq and Syria shall refuse to pay their tribute.

(8) The buildings of Medinah shall reach to Mecca.

The greater signs (*'Alamatu-s-Sa'ah*), seventeen in number, are as follows:

(1) The sun's rising in the west.

(2) The appearance of the *Dabbatu l-Arz,* or "beast" which shall rise out of the earth, in the temple of Mecca or on Mount Safa. This beast is a conglomerate beast with parts resembling various creatures such as a bull, a hog, an elephant, a stag, an ostrich, a lion, a tiger, a cat, a ram, a camel, and an ass. It will appear three times and bring with it the rod of Moses and the seal of Solomon. With Moses' rod it will place a mark of *mu'min* (believer) on the believers, and with the seal, a *kafir* (infidel) for those destined for destruction.

(3) War with the Romans or Greeks, during which time the Antichrist will appear.

(4) The coming of *al Masihu 'd Dajjal,* "the false or lying Christ" (Antichrist). He will be identified by the letters KFR, signifying *kafir,* (infidel), and will be slain by Jesus, who will encounter him at the gate of Lud.

(5) The descent of Jesus on earth for the purpose of killing the Antichrist, reigning forty years before burial at Medinah. Under Him there will be great security and plenty, all hatred and malice being laid aside; when lions and camels, bears and sheep shall live in peace, and a child shall play with serpents unhurt.

(6) War with the Jews.

(7) The appearance of Gog and Magog.

(8) A smoke which shall fill the whole earth.

(9) Three specific lunar eclipses, one to be seen in the east, another in the west, and the third in Arabia.

(10) A reign of one hundred years of gross ignorance when

Arabs will return to the worship of al-Lat and al-'Uzza
and the rest of their ancient idols.

(11) A drying up of the River Euphrates and the discovery
in its bed of a vast heap of gold and silver.

(12) The demolition of the Ka'bah in Mecca by the Ethi-
opians.

(13) The speaking of beasts and inanimate things.

(14) The breaking out of fire in the province of al-Hijaz, or,
according to others, in the Yemen.

(15) The appearance of a man of the descendants of Kahtan,
who shall drive men before him with his staff.

(16) The coming of the *Mahdi* (the Director), who shall
fill the earth with righteousness. The Shi'as consider
him to be the reincarnation of the twelfth Iman,
Mohammed Abu'l Qasem.

(17) A wind which shall sweep away the souls of all who
have but a grain of faith in their hearts (26. 539,540).

The actual Day of Resurrection will be ushered in with a
blast of a trumpet; a great earthquake that will ruin the cities and
level the mountains; a darkening of the sun; a falling of the stars;
a drying up of the oceans (37. 81); the destruction of those not
favored by God, the last to die being the *Malak 'l-Maut* (the
angel of death) (1 Cor. 15:26).

Forty years after this, another sounding of the trumpet will
be accomplished by the angel Asrafil, who, together with Gabriel
and Michael, standing on the Dome of the Rock (*As-Sakhrah*),
shall call together all the bones of all mankind to the resurrection,
Mohammed himself being the first to rise.

The Judgment Day will be a thousand years (37. 32:4). An
alternate verse states fifty thousand years for the period of the
Day of Judgment (37. 70:4). This general resurrection will be
for the righteous as well as for the wicked, distinction being made
in their destiny, the former to an eternity of bliss in the garden of
Ferdaus (Paradise) wherein flow rivers of water which corrupt
not (37. 47:16,17); the latter to *an-Nar* (the fire) of *Jahannam*
(hell) (37. 15:44), prepared for all who follow Satan, "to dwell

therein for ever" (37. 9:69). Man's works will be the criteria in the Judgment. His good works will be placed on the balance that overhangs Paradise, and his evil deeds in the scale that overhangs Hell. The heavier side will be submerged into what lies below and there will be no recourse to appeal nor desire to complain.

3. ANGELS. Angels are superior beings, created of light, endowed with life, speech, and reason; they are sanctified from carnal desire and anger, and obedient to God's commands. Muslims recognize four archangels, or *Karubiyun* (Cherubim), namely, *Jabrail* (Gabriel), the angel of revelation; *Asrafil,* the angel that will sound the trumpet on the Day of Resurrection; *Mikail* (Michael), the patron of the Israelites; and *Izrail* the angel of death.

Every believer is said to be attended by two recording angels called the *Kiramu 'l-katibin,* one of whom records the good deeds, and the other the evil. There are also two angels called *Munkar* and *Nakir,* who examine all the dead in their graves. The chief angel who has charge of hell is called *Malik,* and has several subordinates.

Angels are believed to have intercessory prerogatives (37. 42:3); to act as guardians (37. 13:12; 3:120; 6:61); to uphold the throne of God (37. 69:17); to supervise hell (37. 74:30,31); and to exorcise *jinn* or evil angels, who are of a different species.

4. THE SCRIPTURES. The "Holy Scripture," "Holy Writing," "Holy Book," or "The Word of God," are all terms generally understood by Muslims to refer to the Koran, but more correctly include all books acknowledged by Mohammed to be divinely inspired writings. The number of sacred books delivered to mankind is said to have been 104; of these, 10 were given to Adam, 50 to Seth (a name not mentioned in the Koran), 30 to Enoch, 10 to Abraham, the Torah to Moses, the Zabur to David, the Injil (Gospel) to Jesus, and the Koran to Mohammed. The Muslim further believes that all that is necessary to know of these inspired writings is supposed to have been retained in the Koran (26. 475).

Though Islam grants special honor to the Scriptures other

than the Koran, the belief is widely held that both the Old and
New Testaments have been corrupted, especially the parts that
deal with outstanding differences in theology and doctrine and
those sections that are supposed to have foretold the coming of
the Prophet of Islam.

5. THE PROPHETS. The Arabic word *Nabi* for prophet is a
cognate of Hebrew, which Gesenius says means "one who bub-
bles forth" as a fountain. According to Muslim thought, a *Nabi*
is anyone directly inspired by God, or called by God.

Mohammed is related to have said (8:XXIV:3) that there
were 124,000 prophets, and 315 apostles or messengers, only 28
of whom are mentioned in the Koran. Nine of the latter are
entitled *Ulu 'l-'Azam,* or "possessors of constancy," namely,
Noah, Abraham, David, Jacob, Joseph, Job, Moses, Jesus, and
Mohammed. Six are dignified with special titles: Adam, *Safiyu
'llah,* the Chosen of God; Noah, *Nabiyu 'llah,* the Prophet of
God; Abraham, *Khalilu 'llah,* the Friend of God; Moses, *Kalimu
'llah,* the Converser with God; Jesus, *Ruhu 'llah,* the Spirit of
God; and Mohammed, *Rasulu 'llah,* the Messenger of God.

FIVE PILLARS OF FAITH:

There are five obligatory duties incumbent on all Muslims:
confession of faith, prayers, alms-giving, fasting, and pilgrimage
to Mecca.

1. CONFESSION OF FAITH (*Shahada*). The verbal audible
recitation of the confession of faith is required for acceptance
into Islam: *La ilaha illa l'Lah, wa Muhammadu Rasulu-l'Lah*
(There is no god but God, and Mohammed is His Messenger).
It must be recited, not by rote, but meditatively, purposively, with
a full understanding of its meaning and with an assent from the
heart. It is of interest to note that the entire *Shahada* does not
appear in the Koran as such. The first and second parts appear
repeatedly, but not necessarily as component parts of one testimony. From the earliest dawn of consciousness, every child born
to Muslim parents hears the *Shahada* along with a repetition of

Allahu-Akbar (God is most great) in the call to prayer five times a day.

2. PRAYER (*Salat*). The obligatory worship of God consists of five daily prayers preceded by necessary ceremonial ablutions (*wuzu'*). Although the Koran (37:30:17,18) expressly mentions only four, the actual practice of the Prophet was five: before sunrise (*fajr*), noon (*zuhr*), late afternoon (*'asr*), sunset (*maghrib*), and about two hours later (*'isha*). Before each of the five prayer services the *mu'azan* gives the call to prayer, called the *azan* (*adan,* and *mu'adan,* above):

> God is most great (four times, called the *takbir*):—
> I testify that there is no god but God (two times);
> and I testify that Mohammed is the apostle of God (two times);
> Come to prayer (two times);
> Come to prosperity (two times);
> Prayer is better than sleep (two times before morning prayer only);
> God is most great (two times);
> There is no god but God.

In response to these calls to prayer, the prayers are all public and collective, although under necessity individual prayers are repeated. Each service, led by an *Imam,* is offered facing the *Ka'bah* (*qiblah*) in Mecca and consists of two or more genuflections (*rak'at*). Under special circumstances such as illness, journey, or war, modification or limited postponement is allowed. On Fridays, instead of the noon prayer, a congregational prayer is offered in the mosque and includes a sermon (*khutba*). Special congregational prayers are offered in the middle of the morning on the two festival days called *'ids,* one immediately following the month of fasting and the other following the pilgrimage. Although not ordained as an obligatory duty, individual devotional prayers, especially during the night are emphasized (51. XII:663,664).

By this requirement of the prayers, the Muslim is called—in the midst of his daily duties or on a trip when the bus will stop and all passengers will unite in corporate prayers—to remember that God alone is worthy of worship and to prostrate himself before Him. This is not to be dismissed by the non-Muslim as a meaningless ritual. The psychological and spiritual significance of the prayers must be obvious to any observer.

3. ALMS-GIVING (*Zakat*). Being a social obligation, the terms "almsgiving" and "performing the worship" are linked together about twenty times in the Koran as a kind of formula describing those who have entered Islam. This ordinance, on the one hand, proves the correctness of private property, for you cannot give if you do not own. This fact is pointed out by some as a usual Islamic argument against Communism (37. 37). On the other hand it suggests that property is not owned in the correct way unless payment of *zakat* is made. It serves at the same time to emphasize to the alms-giver that he is *not* owner, but steward of a portion of God's possessions. The amount given varies for different categories: on grains and fruits it is 10 percent if watered by rain, 5 if watered by irrigation; and 2.5 percent on money is prescribed. Money so obtained is to be spent primarily on the poor and the needy. Besides these legal alms, the giving of charities (*sadaqat*) is stressed in the Koran and Traditions.

4. FASTING (*Saum*). The fast is a Koranic injunction (41: 2:183-185) that is to be observed throughout the entire month of Ramadan. It is binding on all adult Muslims of both sexes, save for the aged, sick, pregnant women, nursing mothers, and travelers. No food or drink is to pass down the throat from the break of dawn to sunset. Even the swallowing of one's saliva, or the insertion of medicine in ear or nose or head wound, or an injection, is considered as invalidating the fast. The thoughts of self-discipline and penitence are also prominent. Muslim journals stress the spiritual value of the fast. The universality of the fast is enforced in many countries.

5. PILGRIMAGE (*Hajj*). This is the fifth practice incumbent on every Muslim to perform once in a lifetime provided he can support himself during the journey and can also arrange for the provision of his dependents during his absence. The pilgrimage

ceremonial begins every year on the seventh and ends on the tenth of the month of *Dhu 'l-Hijjah.* When the pilgrim is about six miles from the holy city, he enters upon the state of *ihram:* he casts off, after prayers, his ordinary clothes and puts on two seamless garments; he walks almost barefooted and neither shaves, cuts his hair nor cuts his nails. The principal activity consists of a visit to the sacred mosque (*al-Masjid al Haram*); the kissing of the Black Stone (*al-Hajar al-Aswad*); seven circumambulations of the Ka'bah, three times running and four times slowly; the visit to the sacred stone called *Maqam Ibrahim;* the ascent of and running between Mount Safa and Mount Marwa seven times; the visit to Mount Arafat; the hearing of a sermon there and spending the night at Muzdalifa; the throwing of stones at the three pillars at Mina and offering sacrifice on the last day of *ihram,* which is the *'id* of sacrifice (*'Id al-Adha*) (62. XII: 664).

The sense of community is particularly strong when Muslims from all over the world converge at the holy places for the *Hajj.*

Crucial Doctrinal Difficulties Between Muslims and Christians

1. GOD. As we have already mentioned, the "Allah" of the Muslim is the same Being as the "God" of the Christian, however, there are differences that one needs to bear in mind. Islam, like Christianity (and Judaism) is strictly monotheistic. Each recognizes only one God (Deut. 6:4; Mark 12:29; Koran, 2:255; 6: 103), but each stresses a different aspect of the One God: Judaism the holiness of God; Christianity the love of God; and Islam the omnipotence and greatness of God. In the last, the free will of God is unhampered and unrestrained by any limitation— human or otherwise—hence, a Muslim's idea of God seems inconsistent to us, for what he believes God wills one day may be reversed the next. This, in fact is the basis of their doctrine of abrogation with regard to verses in the Koran which seem contradictory to us: "Verses which we (God) abrogate or cause them to be forgotten, We bring a better [in its stead] or a similar

one. Knowest thou not that God is able to do all things?" (37. 2:100). To a Muslim, anthropomorphisms or likening God to man in any way is blasphemy.

To the Muslim, Christian representation of God in sculpture or picture appear highly inconsistent, especially in view of the first two commandments of the Decalogue:

> Thou shalt have no other gods before me. Thou shalt not make unto thee any graven image, or any likeness of any thing that is in heaven above, or that is in the earth beneath, or that is in the water under the earth: Thou shalt not bow down thyself to them, nor serve them; for I the Lord thy God am a jealous God, visiting the iniquity of the fathers upon the children unto the third and fourth generation of them that hate me; and shewing mercy unto thousands of them that love me, and keep my commandments (Ex. 20:3-6).

2. HOLY SPIRIT.   The Koran (37. 16:102) teaches that this expression refers to a medium or an angel through whom truth was brought down, somewhat similar to Hebrews 1:14 ("are they not all ministering spirits?"). In Mohammed Marmeduke Pickthall's *Meaning of the Glorious Koran,* he explains the expression in a footnote as being the angel Gabriel. When Christians equate the Holy Spirit with the third person of the Godhead, a Muslim puts his fingers in his ears, lest blasphemy enter in his soul. He cannot understand why an angel is put on a level with Allah (38. 74).

3. SCRIPTURE.   The fact and number of Scripture have been dealt with under the Five Articles of Faith (page 83). The doctrine of abrogation was referred to above as a prerogative of God. Here we deal with inspiration and corruption of Scripture and the question of the Hadith or Tradition.

There is a vast amount of difference among Christians as to inspiration. It is no wonder that the Muslims would also have varying views on the subject. Verbal inspiration of the Koran, however, is a fundamental tenet of Islam. They recognize two kinds or levels of inspiration, *wahy zahir* (external inspiration) and *wahy batin* (internal inspiration). The former was the verbal transmission of the literal text of the Koran from the mouth of the angel Gabriel to the ear of the Prophet. Internal inspiration is that which the Prophet obtained by thought and analogical reasoning, just as the *Mujtahidun,* or enlightened doctors of the law obtain it (26. 213).

Specific instruction is given in the Koran to the believers:

> Believe in God and his messenger and the Scripture which he has revealed unto his messenger, and the scripture which he revealed aforetime. Who ever disbelieves in God and his angels and his scriptures and his messengers and the last day, he verily has wandered far astray (37. 4:136).

Despite this seemingly unequivocal command to believe the Scriptures that were revealed *aforetime* (i.e., the Torah, Zabur, and Injil) of which God declares Himself to be the guardian (37. 15:9), there is the widely held belief that all have been corrupted by the Jews and Christians. The Arabic term *tahrif* is explained to mean "to change, alter, or turn aside anything from the truth" (26. 61). Muslim controversialists when faced with the "unreconcilable" contents of the Koran vis-a-vis the former Scriptures charge their forerunners with having corrupted them.

The Hadith (Tradition) is a divine saying, or a tradition that relates a revelation from God in the language of the Prophet. An example is quoted from the *Mishkat:* "Abu Hurairah said, 'The Prophet of God related these words of God, "The sons of Adam vex me, and abuse the age, whereas I am The AGE itself: In my hands are all events: I have made the day and night" ' " (8. book i, ch. i. pt. 1.).

There is much in the life of Mohammed and in the teachings of the Koran that we can accept. The difficulty comes in this Hadith, which is a system of teaching built on "authentic" traditions passed on regarding what Mohammed said or did regarding particular questions—how he washed his hands, how he combed his hair, his likes and dislikes—which have become important patterns of life for the faithful Muslim. To imitate the Prophet was the highest goal piety could aim at (19. 3,22). The acts of the Prophet legitimized them in the lives of his followers. The system of thought that developed as a result was known as the *Sunna:* the way of life of Mohammed which became the way of life of Islam. The authentic chain of transmission of this *Sunna* forms the Hadith, whose accent shifted to a great extent from the revelation of the *Book* to the *person* of Mohammed.

Muslim thought leaders recognize this problem, as Fazlur Rahman states:

> Unless, therefore, the problem of the Hadith is critically, historically and constructively treated, there seems little prospect of distinguishing the essential from the purely historical. But it is precisely this task which the "Ulama" are resolutely refusing to do. They fear that if Hadith is thus exposed to a scientific investigation, the concept of the "Sunna of the Prophet," the second pillar of Islam besides the Qur'ān, will be destroyed and that it would then be impossible to hold on to the Qur'ān as well; for that which anchors the Qur'ān *is* the Sunna of the Prophet. Some of the recent Muslim and non-Muslim wholesale and absolute rejections of Hadith and the Prophetic Sunna undoubtedly strengthen these fears (39. 310,311).

It cannot be denied that a part of the difficulty in evangelizing Muslims lies in their great dependence on and belief in the Traditions that have far exceeded the Koran in quantity and almost in importance.

4. SATAN.   The Koran not only mentions Satan, it gives a full description of his fall in Sura the Heights (37. 10:17). The Muslim's explanation of the origin of evil is very simple—God is the cause of everything, of evil as well as good. This fatalistic concept, of course, prevents a Muslim from feeling guilt or remorse. The problem of sin, as we know it, then, does not exist in Islam. Therefore, redemption and salvation all have entirely different aspects. That is not to say that "sin" doesn't exist in Islam, for there is pardonable as well as unpardonable sin in their theology. The most heinous sin—the unpardonable—is *shirk,* the attributing of a partner or other god to God the Creator!

Verily, God will not forgive the union of other gods with Himself! But other than this will He forgive to whom He pleaseth. And He who uniteth gods with God hath devised a great wickedness (37. 4:51).

Because of misrepresentation of the Christian doctrine of the Trinity, Christians have been accused of practicing *shirk*. The Muslim believes in the sinlessness of Christ, but the difficulty arises in his belief that *all* the prophets were sinless. Regarding sin, Bethmann summarizes:

> Naturally, as there is no deep conviction of sin in Islam, no feeling of an estrangement between God and man, there is no need for reconciliation, no need for redemption, nor for a Saviour from sin, no need for a complete turn in life, nor for being born again in the likeness of the Spirit. And here lies the deepest gulf which separates Christianity from Islam. (5. 80).

5. PREDESTINATION. *Taqdir* in Arabic, is usually considered to be the sixth of what we have called the Five Articles of Faith. It is the absolute decree of good and evil, and the orthodox believe that whatever has, or shall, come to pass in this world proceeds entirely from the Divine Will, and has been irrevocably fixed and recorded on a preserved tablet by the pen of fate (37. 472). This does not mean, however, that there is no room for personal accountability (37. 18:28-30; 13:18,20-22), or that the Muslim, in the words of Bethmann, "will fold his hands, settling down to await the raven of Allah to feed him" (5. 77). "Fatalism," he continues, "does not mean inactivity or laziness, as it is often pictured by Western tourists. It is rather an unconcern over the final outcome, an unconcern borne by the keen sense of God's absolute sovereignty and man's complete dependence upon God" (5. 77).

6. STATE OF THE DEAD.

> They ask thee of the Hour: when will it come to port?
> Why (ask they)? What hast thou to tell thereof?
> Unto thy Lord belongeth (knowledge of) the term thereof.

Thou art but a warner unto him who feareth it.
On the day when they behold it, it will be as if they had but
tarried for an evening or the morn thereof. (37. 79:42-
56).

From the above verses and others on the subject of the state
of the dead, it is quite apparent that Mohammed had a clear
understanding of the unconsciousness of the soul after death.
According to Koranic teachings, there is no intermediate state
between the day of death and the day of resurrection. There is
no purgatory, no heavenly abode where the soul leads a conscious
existence. The moment a person dies, he becomes entirely unconscious and unaware of what is going on in the world; but
when the day of resurrection is ushered in with the sound of the
trumpet, it will appear to him that he had been separated from
his family but a single night. The commentator on the Koran
Abdullah Yusuf Ali says regarding the state of the dead:

Death is like sleep and may be compared to the evening of life.
In sleep we do not know how the time passes. When we wake up
from the sleep of death at the resurrection we shall not know
whether it was the following moment or the following hour after
we slept, but we shall feel that it is morning, for we shall be conscious of all that goes on, as one awakened in the morning (1.
II:1685).

As for the time of death, the Koran teaches that when an
individual reaches the age which God has appointed for him he
is overtaken by death, which he can neither put off nor hasten
(37. 16:61); and when he dies his *Ruh* (spirit) ascends to God
(37. 70:4), a doctrine almost identical to that taught in the
Bible: "Then shall the dust return to the earth as it was: and
the spirit shall return unto God who gave it" (Eccl. 12:7). It
is of interest to note that both Egyptians and Babylonians were
firm believers in the consciousness of the dead and provided food
and drink for their departed loved ones; whereas, Mohammed emphasized the fact that the dead cannot come back to this earth
as is also clearly stated in Ecclesiastes:

For the living know that they shall die: but the dead know not any thing, neither have they any more a reward; for the memory of them is forgotten. Also their love, and their hatred, and their envy, is now perished; neither have they any more a portion for ever in any thing that is done under the sun. (Eccl. 9:5, 6).

7. DIET AND HEALTH.

O ye who believe! Strong drink and games of chance and idols and divining arrows are only an infamy of Satan's handiwork. Leave it aside in order that ye may succeed. Satan seeketh only to cast among you enmity and hatred by means of strong drink and games of chance, and to turn you from remembrance of Allah and from (His) worship. Will ye then have done? (37. 5:90,91).

All countries under Muslim rule are officially "dry," in respect of the clear command and admonition of the Prophet. Concerning food, also, clear distinction is made between the clean and unclean meats, almost identical with the biblical injunction in Genesis 9:4 and Leviticus 11.

O mankind! Eat of that which is lawful and wholesome in the earth, and follow not the footsteps of the devil. Lo! he is an open enemy for you. . . . O ye who believe! Eat of the good things wherewith We have provided you, and render thanks to Allah if it is (indeed) He whom ye worship. He hath forbidden you only carrion, and blood, and swineflesh, and that which hath been immolated to (the name of) any other than Allah. But he who is driven by necessity, neither craving nor transgressing, it is no sin for him. Lo! Allah is Forgiving, Merciful (37. 2:168, 172,173. *See also* 5:3-5; 6:118-21; 16:114-18).

Mohammed allowed Muslims to eat foods that were considered lawful to the "People of the Book." No doubt he meant by this both the Jews and Christians, for he knew that the Jews would not eat blood nor unclean foods, and that the Christians abstained from meats offered to idols, from blood, and from strangled animals (Acts 15:29).

PROBLEMS CONNECTED WITH THE PERSON OF CHRIST:

To the Buddhist, the Shintoist, the Taoist, and the Hindu, Christ is a stranger. Not so in the case of the Muslim! He considers Christ as highly exalted, a "Sign" to the worlds, a spirit from God, the messenger of God, illustrious in this world and in the next—but otherwise He is considered to be on the same level as any other prophet. Bethmann writes:

> By no other religion is Christ's position challenged in such a definite manner as it is in Islam. Therefore, everything depends upon our right representation of Christ. If we are able to represent Christ in His full spiritual power, every other problem will be solved. And here lies the crux of the matter (5. 249).

The traditional conflict between Christians and Muslims centers in the divinity of Christ (His two natures), His preexistence, incarnation, Sonship, creatorship, crucifixion, and substitutionary sacrifice. The Christian Church for centuries has defended her creed against these attacks. In the course of this undertaking, her champions have tried to find similes, metaphors, and symbols in order to "prove" convincingly the truth of these doctrines. But in spite of this amassing of volumes of proof, texts, and unanswerable arguments, the Church has failed to make any measurable impact on Islam. No amount of discussion and argument over these points has ever or will ever convince anybody against his will, because the truth of these doctrines does not lie on the intellectual level where it can be reached by the power of reasoning. It lies on the spiritual level to which we find entrance by listening quietly to the Spirit of God, who is willing to reveal Himself to everybody, Muslim and Christian alike (5. 250).

After all, does not the Apostle Paul recognize that "the preaching of the cross is to them that perish foolishness" (1 Cor. 1:18), and that preaching itself is "foolishness," nevertheless an instrument ordained by God to save "them that believe" (vs. 21)? Is it any wonder then, that "the things of the Spirit of God" should seem to be "foolishness" (1 Cor. 2:14) and unreasonable to the Muslim? Hence the futility of trying to convert Muslims by reasoning, for we must be the first to recognize that the incarnation, life, death and resurrection of Christ were certainly of all things the most unreasonable! When will we accept the vanity of "proof" and "argument," and humbly rely on the Spirit of God to bring conviction, as we become ambassadors of God to establish a *koinonia,* a fellowship of mutual confidence and trust founded on love and respect? But there is at long last a sound of a rustling in the tops of the mulberry trees (2 Sam. 5:24) as different scattered attempts are being made to understand the Muslim for what he is and for what he believes, to find common ground and dialogue with him in the philosophy of the Apostle Paul:

> I have freely and happily become a servant of any and all so that I can win them to Christ. When I am with the Jews I seem as one of them so that they will listen to the Gospel and I can win them to Christ. When I am with Gentiles who follow Jewish customs and ceremonies I don't argue, even though I don't agree, because I want to help them.
>
> When with the heathen I agree with them as much as I can, except of course that I must always do what is right as a Christian. And so, by agreeing, I can win their confidence and help them too.
>
> When I am with those whose consciences bother them easily, I don't act as though I know it all and don't say they are foolish; the result is that they are willing to let me help them. Yes, whatever a person is like, I try to find common ground with him so that he will let me tell him about Christ and let Christ save him (1 Cor. 9:19-22, Taylor's Translation).

Appendix A

Ethnological Table of Nations

Descendants of Noah

1 1 JAPHETH
2 . 1 Gomer
3 . . 1 Ashkenaz
4 . . 2 Riphath
5 . . 3 Togarmah
6 . 2 Magog
7 . 3 Madia
8 . 4 Javan
9 . . 1 Elishah
10 . . 2 Tarshish
11 . . 3 Kittim
12 . . 4 Dodan(im)
13 . 5 Tubal
14 . 6 Meshech
15 . 7 Tiras
16 2 HAM
17 . 1 Cush
18 . . 1 Seba
19 . . 2 Havilah
20 . . 3 Sabta(h)
21 . . 4 Raamah
22 . . . . 1 Sheba
23 . . . . 2 Dedan
24 . . 5 Sabtec(h)a
25 . . 6 Nimrod

```
26 . 2 Mizraim
27 . . 1 Lud(im)
28 . . 2 Anam(im)
29 . . 3 Lehab(im)
30 . . 4 Naphtuh(im)
31 . . 5 Pathrus(im)
32 . . 6 Casluh(im)
33 . . 7 Caphtor(im)
34 . 3 Put (Phut)
35 . 4 Canaan
36 . . 1 Sidon
37 . . 2 Heth
38 . . 3 Jebus(ite)
39 . . 4 Amor(ite)
40 . . 5 Girgash(ite)
41 . . 6 Hiv(ite)
42 . . 7 Ark(ite)
43 . . 8 Sin(ite)
44 . . 9 Arvad(ite)
45 . . 10 Zemar(ite)
46 . . 11 Hamath(ite)
47 3 SHEM
48 . 1 Elam
49 . 2 Asshur
50 . 3 Arpachshad
51 . . 1 Shelah
52 . . . . 1 Eber
53 . . . . . 1 Peleg
54 . . . . . . 2 Joktan
55 . . . . . . 1 Almodad
56 . . . . . . 2 Sheleph
57 . . . . . . 3 Hazarmaveth
58 . . . . . . 4 Jerah
59 . . . . . . 5 Hadoram
60 . . . . . . 6 Uzal
61 . . . . . . 7 Diklah
62 . . . . . . 8 Obal
```

63 . . . . 9 Abimael
64 . . . . 10 Sheba
65 . . . . 11 Ophir
66 . . . . 12 Havilah
67 . . . . 13 Jobab
68 . . . . . . 1 Reu
69 . . . . 1 Serug
70 . . . . 1 Nahor
71 . . . . 1 Terah
72 . . . . 1 Haran
73 . . . . 1 Lot
74 . . . . 0 Milcah (wife of Nahor)
75 . . . . 0 Iscah
76 . . . . 2 Nahor
77 . . . . Milcah
78 . . . . 1 Uz
79 . . . . 2 Buz
80 . . . . 3 Kemuel
81 . . . . 1 Aram
82 . . . . 4 Chesed
83 . . . . 5 Hazo
84 . . . . 6 Pildash
85 . . . . 7 Jidlaph
86 . . . . 8 Bethuel
87 . . . . 0 Rebecca
88 . . . . Reumah
89 . . . . 9 Tebah
90 . . . . 10 Gaham
91 . . . . 11 Tahash
92 . . . . 12 Maacah
93 . . . . 3 Abram
94 . . . . 0 Sarai
95 . . . . Hagar
96 . . . . 1 Ishmael
97 . . . . 1 Nebaioth
98 . . . . 2 Kedar
99 . . . . 3 Adbeel

```
100 . . . . . . . . . . . . . .  4 Mibsam
101 . . . . . . . . . . . . . .  5 Mishma
102 . . . . . . . . . . . . . .  6 Dumah
103 . . . . . . . . . . . . . .  7 Massa
104 . . . . . . . . . . . . . .  8 Hadar(d)
105 . . . . . . . . . . . . . .  9 Tema
106 . . . . . . . . . . . . . . 10 Jetur
107 . . . . . . . . . . . . . . 11 Naphish
108 . . . . . . . . . . . . . . 12 Kedemah
109 . . . . . . . . . . . . . .  0 Bashemath  (Mahalath)
110 . . . . . . . . . . . . . Sarah
111 . . . . . . . . . . . . .  2 Isaac
112 . . . . . . . . . . . . . Rebecca
113 . . . . . . . . . . . . .  2 Jacob
114 . . . . . . . . . . . . . . Rachel
115 . . . . . . . . . . . . . . 11 Joseph
116 . . . . . . . . . . . . . . 12 Benjamin
117 . . . . . . . . . . . . . . Bilhah
118 . . . . . . . . . . . . . .  5 Dan
119 . . . . . . . . . . . . . .  6 Naphtali
120 . . . . . . . . . . . . . . Leah
121 . . . . . . . . . . . . . .  1 Reuben
122 . . . . . . . . . . . . . .  2 Simeon
123 . . . . . . . . . . . . . .  3 Levi
124 . . . . . . . . . . . . . .  4 Judah
125 . . . . . . . . . . . . . .  9 Issachar
126 . . . . . . . . . . . . . . 10 Zebulun
127 . . . . . . . . . . . . . .  0 Dinah
128 . . . . . . . . . . . . . . Zilpah
129 . . . . . . . . . . . . . .  7 Gad
130 . . . . . . . . . . . . . .  8 Asher
131 . . . . . . . . . . . . . 1 Esau  (Edom-Seir)
132 . . . . . . . . . . . . . . Adah (Hittite)
133 . . . . . . . . . . . . . .  1 Eliphaz
134 . . . . . . . . . . . . . . .  1 Teman
135 . . . . . . . . . . . . . . .  2 Omar
136 . . . . . . . . . . . . . . .  3 Zepho(i)
```

137 . . . . 4 Gatam
138 . . . . 5 Kenaz
139 . . . . Timnah
140 . . . . 6 Amalek
141 . . . . Bashemath (Ishmael's d.)
142 . . . . 2 Reuel
143 . . . . 1 Nahath
144 . . . . 2 Zerah
145 . . . . 3 Shammah
146 . . . . 4 Mizzah
147 . . . . Aholibamah (Hivite)
148 . . . . 3 Jeush
149 . . . . 4 Jaalam
150 . . . . 5 Korah
151 . . . . Keturah
152 . . . . 3 Zimran
153 . . . . 4 Jokshan
154 . . . . 1 Sheba
155 . . . . 2 Dedan
156 . . . . 1 Asshurim
157 . . . . 2 Letushim
158 . . . . 3 Leummim
159 . . . . 5 Medan
160 . . . . 6 Midian
161 . . . . 1 Ephah
162 . . . . 2 Epher
163 . . . . 3 Hanoch
164 . . . . 4 Abidah
165 . . . . 5 Eldaah
166 . . . . 7 Ishbak
167 . . . . 8 Shuah
168 . 4 Lud
169 . 5 Aram
170 . . 1 Uz
171 . . 2 Hul
172 . . 3 Gether
173 . . 4 Mash

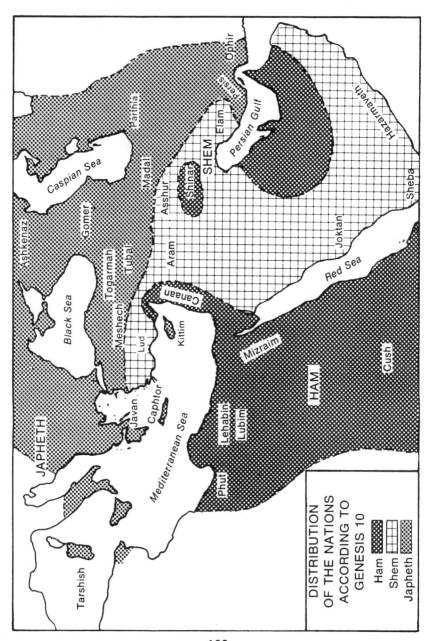

DISTRIBUTION
OF THE NATIONS
ACCORDING TO
GENESIS 10

Ham
Shem
Japheth

Appendix B

Chronology of Events

DATE	EVENT
622	Hijra
632–34	Abu Bakr and wars of *riddah* (secession, apostasy)
632–33	Within six months tribes of Central Arabia united: Tayyi, Asas Ghatafan, Bani Hanifah in al-Yamamah, Bahrayn, Uman, Hadramout, Yaman
633	Syria, Persia
634	Ghassanids on Easter Sunday, Ajnodayn (July 30), Bursa (Old Damascus)
635	Fihl, Damascus, after six-month siege
636	Yarmuk Battle (August 20), Theodosius, brother of Heraclius. Antioch, Aleppo, Chalcis
637	Qadisiya, death of Rustam, Iraq west of Tigris lay open, Ctesiphon (Persian capital)
638	Jerusalem
639–41	Egypt
640	Caesarea, Farama, key to eastern Egypt, Bilbaya (near Cairo), Theodora fled to Alexandria, Cyrus to Babylon on the Nile, Hulwan, Susiana (Khuzistan), Pars, Basrah, Kufah
641	Mawsil (near Nineveh), Egypt completed, Shabshir
642–52	Nahavand (near Ecbatan), Persia
643	Isfahan, Mukran, Baluchistan to borders of India
644, 645	Armenia revolted
645	· Alexandria regained by Manuel, an Armenian

DATE	EVENT
646	Alexandria's second fall
647	Tripoli
649	Cyprus—first maritime victory
650	Arwad
654	Rhodes pillaged
655	Syro-Egyptian fleet destroyed—Byzantine navy of 500 ships
661–750	Umayyad Caliphate
663–71	Khorassan
668, 669	Sicily pillaged
668	Chalcedon
669	Constantinople attacked
670	Qayrawan
672	Rhodes
674	Cyzicus, base of operations vs. Constantinople
692	Justinian II defeated near Cilisian Sebastopolis
693	Berber resistance and Byzantine authority finished in North Africa
698	Carthage, Tangier
699–700	Afghanistan
705	Crossing of Oxus separating Iran from Turan (Persian-speaking and Turkish-speaking)
706–9	Bokhara reconquered
707	Armenia, second time, Tyana (Cappadocia), Sardis, Pergamos
710	Mukran (Baluchistan)
710–12	Samarkand, Khwarazm, Sind (lower Indus)
711	Gibraltar and Iberian Peninsula by Tariq vs. Roderick, last Visigoth
713	Seville, Merida, Saragossa (Caesaraugusta), Jaxartes provinces of Farghanah (Buddhist territories), Multan in south Punjab
715	Kashghai (in Chinese Turkestan)
717–19	Rhodes, second time
717–18	Crossing of Pyrenees
720	Narbonne

DATE	EVENT
721	Toulouse—first failure in Europe, lost the battle
732	Garonne, Bordeaux, Poitiers, Tours—farthest advance in Europe, lost the battle to Charles Martel, Transoxiana, Sind
734	Avignon
743	Lyons
750–1258	Abbasid Caliphate—little territorial expansion during Abbasid period. Unity broken down by splintered sultanies of Persian and Turkish dynasties
756	Umayyads of Cordova, Almoravids, Almohads, Idrisids (Morocco), Aghlabids (Tunis)
759	Narbonne relinquished as a base of operations in Europe
837	Naples
841	Bari—for thirty years main base of operations vs. Italy, Venice
846	Rome threatened, Aghlabids landed at Ostia
872–82	Pope John VIII paid tribute for two years
869	Malta
934, 935	Genoa sacked (from Sicily based forces)
950	Piratical raids through Alpine passes into mid-Europe
1071–91	Norman conquest of Sicily
1071	Battle of Manzikert, Seljuk Turks ruled from India to Mediterranean
1055	Seljuk Turks capture Bagdad, hold Samarkand to Mediterranean, Ghazna and Asia Minor swallowed up. Crusades—beginning of European relations with the Levant: Syria, Palestine, Rhodes, Cyprus, Damietta. Mongols—Ghengis Khan stopped by Mamluks of Egypt in Palestine
1100	Karmatians. Indonesia trade centers at Perlak, Samudra—Pasei of Sumatra, Achin, Malacca, Java
1167–1227	Genghis Khan

DATE   EVENT

Batu succeeded his father, Jochi as Khan of Kipchak, he took over a territory from Aral regions
into Eastern Europe. At his death, his western
frontier ran from the mouth of the Danube
northward by the Carpathians to Kholm and
Lublin and thence northeastward to the Gulf of
Finland and Lake Ladoga

1236–1237   Mongols, under Ogdai invaded Georgia and
Greater Armenia, Tiflis and Kars fell. Com-
mander was Batu, son of Jochi, Ogdai's deceased
elder brother. Bolgari, capital city of Bulgaria
fell. He crossed the Volga, pushed through the
forests of Perga and Tambov and reached
Ryazan which fell December 21, 1237. Inhabitants attrociously ravaged. Batu was awarded
as his fief the vast steppes which stretch from
the Carpathian Mountains to Lake Balkash, with
headquarters on the Volga

1237–42   European campaign under Batu

1241   Moscow, Kazelsk, near Kaluga, and Kiev received
the horrors of Ryazan. Thence Batu went to
ravage Hungary and Baidar and Kaidu to Poland.
At Pest, King Bela IV escaped but was pursued
to Adriatic coast, entire route being pillaged by
the Mongols. Esztergan, on the other side of the
Danube taken by asault on December 25

1243   Genghis Khan routed the Seljuks, put them under
tribute. Ertoghrul and Osman establish Ottoman
Sultanate in Asia Minor

1255   Bereke Khan, son of Batu ravaged Russia. Pope
Alexander IV called for a general crusade against
the Mongols. Christians lacked united front.
Meanwhile a Tatar host, led by Nogai and
Tulabagha appeared in Poland, who took and
destroyed Cracow and advanced to Bytham
(Beuthan) in Oppeln

DATE	EVENT
1258	Hulagu attacked the last Abbasid Caliph of Bagdad. In February they sacked the city. Next came Aleppo. Reconquest of Spain, except Granada. English and French scholars study in Spanish-Arabic universities. Greek-Arabic-Latin translations of literary works at Toledo
1259–94	Kublai Khan
1281–84	Nikudar Ahmad, third Il-Khan, first to become a Moslem
1294–1307	Timur Khan (Tamerlane)
1299	Independence declared by Osman at Yenishehir as Ghazis
1326	Brusa
1331	Nicea
1337	Nicomedia
1345	Cantacuzenus asked Orkhan to help gain throne
1349	Second call for help from Cantacuzenus vs. Stephen Dushan
1350?	Third call for help, robbing of churches to pay Orkhan
1354	Turks cross Hellespont, capture Gallipoli, first aggressive action in Europe
1359–89	Murad I
1362	Adrianople made his capital (moved from Brusa), remained there till fall of Constantinople
1364	Pope Urban V's crusade vs. Murad cut to pieces
1366	Bulgaria fell to Turks
1371	Serbians defeated, September 26. Macedonia, Cavalla, Drama, Serres
1372	Crossed Vadar River. Bosnia, Albania, Greece raided
1382	Eastern Kipchak or White Horde united with Golden Horde and marched into Russia, captured Serpuklov and Moscow (August 23), where he (Toktamish) butchered the inhabitants, plundered and burned. Repeated it in Vladimir,

DATE   EVENT

Zvenigorod, Yuriev, Mozhaisk and Dimitrov, Pereslaul, and Lalamna

1384–85   Sofia captured by Turks

1386   Nish

1389   Revolt of Bosnia, Serbia, Bulgaria. Battle of Kosovo, June 15, South Serbs irretrievably defeated

1390   Azak put to flames by Temur. He spared Muslims, slew natives, which included, with expatriates, Egyptians, Venetians, Genoese, Gobalan, and Basque inhabitants. Tamerlane invades from Transoxiana, Egypt spared. Ottomans face a reborn Persia as rival. Uthman and descendants in early fourteenth century established at western end of Asia Minor. During century they crossed the Bosphorus, encircled Byzantium, reached Danube in Bulgaria, and borders of Albania and Thessaly. Tamerlane brought a temporary setback in Balkan Peninsula, Crimea, Armenia.

1389–1402 Bayezid I Yildirim "Thunderbolt"

1390   Conquest of Asia Minor undertaken. Timur approaching, but turned northward to Russia, Turkestan, Persia, India, Syria (respite of seven years for Ottomans)

1393   Tirnovo, capital of Eastern Bulgaria fell July 17. Wallachia on northern bank of Danube

1394   Karamania (leading Anatolian emirate)

1395   War with Hungary who determined to impose Catholic faith on its Orthodox population. Ottomans granted almost unlimited freedom of religion. Siege of Constantinople begun for eight years till Timur's arrival. Nicopolis, Vidin, Silistria opened the way into Hungary. King Sigismund of Hungary remonstrated, then asked Pope Boniface IX for help who launched crusade vs. Turks.

DATE	EVENT
1396	Crusades assembled at Buda, marched down the Danube, treated the Orthodox as the enemy. At Nicopolis destroyed by Bayezid's and Christian allies
1402	Battle of Ankara, Timur vs. Bayezid. Many Muslims in Timur's ranks
1403	Bayezid committed suicide in March, 1403, while still in captivity
1403–81	Conquest of Balkans. (Empire restored within a decade of 1403)
1403	Timur departs, leaving absolute vacuum in Asia Minor
1413–21	Mohammed I, Bayezid's younger son succeeded to throne
1416	Venetian fleet defeats Turks, honorable peace negotiated
1421–51	Murad I
1422	Siege of Constantinople failed
1425	Manuel II died. Successor John VIII was stripped of all but walls of Constantinople
1430	Saloniki captured from Venice
1439	Serbia reconquered
1441–43	John Hunyadi, leader of crusade called by Pope Eugenius defeated Turks in Serbia and advanced to Sofia
1444	Ten-year truce signed in June. Murad to Asia Minor. Pope broke the truce and resumed the crusade, defeated at Battle of Varna, November 10. Repetition of Nicopolis
1448	Second Battle of Kosova, Hunyadi defeated (as in 1389)
1450	Gutenburg invents printing with metal, movable type
1451–81	Mohammed II
1453	Fall of Constantinople, May 29. Kaffa, Sudak, Balaklava and Inkerman in the Crimea fell to

Date	Event
	the troops of Mohammed who restored Mengli Girai, the deposed Mongol Khan, who raided Lithuania and Poland
1455	Syria, Palestine, Egypt and North Africa to Algeria fall to Turks
1455–58	Pope Calistus III
1456	John Hunyadi defeated Turks at Belgrade, preventing their conquest of Hungary for seventy years
1458–64	Pope Pius I
1459	Serbia (except Belgrade) became Turkish pashalik
1463	Bosnia
1464–71	Pope Paul II
1468	Albania
1469	Spain united under Ferdinand of Aragon and Isabella of Castille
1456	Greece proper
1460	Peloponnesus
1471–84	Pope Sixtus IV
1478	Mohammed II stopped by John Hunyadi at Belgrade and by Skanderbeg in Albania. Spanish Inquisition instituted by Ferdinand and Isabella
1479	Venetians defeated
1480	Otranto falls to Turks
1481–1512	Bayezid II
1483	Birth of Luther. Fall of Herzegovina
1484–92	Pope Innocent VIII
1488	Bartholomew Diaz, Portuguese, discovers Cape of Good Hope, sea-route opens to India
1489–1556	Thomas Cranmer
1489–1565	Guillaume Farel
1491–1556	Ignatius Loyola, founder of Jesuits, chief instrument of Catholic Counter-Reformation
1492–1503	Pope Alexander VI
1492	Columbus discovers America
1497	Expulsion of Jews from Portugal who refused Catholic conversion

DATE	EVENT
1498	Vasco da Gama reaches India via Cape of Good Hope. May 22 he entered Calicut harbor. Portugal took Alexandrian trade. Turks lost naval superiority outside Mediterranean.
1499	Battle of Lepanto, Turks defeated Venice
1500	Ottoman supremacy in eastern Mediterranean to last 300 years, vs. the combined forces of Venice, Spain, and Papacy
1503–1513	Pope Julius II
1512–20	Selim I
1513–22	Pope Leo X
1514	Persians defeated, Kurdistan added to Ottoman Empire
1516	Syria at Marj-Dobik, August 23
1517	Beginning of Reformation, Luther's theses at Wittenberg
1519	Charles V began reign as emperor
1519–22	Ferdinand Magellan circumnavigated the globe
1520–66	Suleiman the Magnificent
1520	Luther burns papal bull, earns wrath of Charles, excommunicated by Leo X
1521	Mohammed Girai Khan, devastated country, massacred the people, desecrated the churches en route to Moscow where he negotiated a treaty with Grand Prince Basil for a perpetual tribute to the Krim Khan. Belgrade surrenders to Turks August 29, opens road to Hungary
1522	Rhodes, last outpost of militant Christendom in eastern Mediterranean, falls July 28
1522–23	Pope Adrian VI, last non-Italian pope
1522	Diet of Nurnberg, dealt with aid for war vs. Turks
1523–34	Pope Clement VII, efforts at reform inconclusive, ended in sack of Rome and his imprisonment in the castle of Saint Angelo
1525	Babur, great grandson of Timur, invades India, Afghanistan, Deccan, Bengal, and Kashmir. Charles V defeats French and Italians at **Pavia**,

DATE	EVENT
	Francis I taken prisoner, appeals to Suleiman to attack Charles V, head of the House of Hapsburg.
1526	Diet of Speyers failed to enforce Edict of Worms. Adjourned August 27. Battle of Mohacs (August 29). Hungarians suffered fatal defeat. Suleiman put John Zapolya on Hungarian throne, after killing King Louis of Hungary, brother-in-law of Charles V.
1527	Zapolya killed, replaced by Ferdinand, Charles's brother. Sack of Rome by Charles V and capture of Pope Clement VII
1529	Germany invaded by Turks. Siege of Vienna, September 28. Torrential rains. Turks retreat on October 14. Beginning of the end of Turkish military supremacy. Protest of the Princes, April 19
1530	Diet of Augsburg, and death sentence on Protestantism
1532	Turkish forces had actually left Constantinople on April 25, reportedly headed toward Hungary. Charles V pleaded on May 6 with a counter offer to the Schmalkaldian League, and made concessions to the Lutherans. On August 26, Suleiman ordered his forces to return to Constantinople. By then the Lutherans had obtained concessions. The terms of Nurnberg formed the rally point of Protestant demands for almost ten years and were of primary importance for the survival, expansion, and consolidation of Lutheranism in Germany. It is paradoxical that an invading army of Muslims should have contributed so much to the cause of Protestantism in its crucial formative stage. When Charles's next opportunity to intervene came, fifteen years later, the Protestants were so thoroughly established that force could achieve little or nothing

DATE	EVENT
1533	Turkish-Austrian peace treaty with Ferdinand. Terms: Zapolya remain king of Hungary, Ferdinand, keep one-third of country he occupied at the time. Khaireddin Barbarosa appointed Kapudan Pasha, thereby combining North African Muslim sea power with Ottoman Empire. Defeated combined naval forces of Europe. Clement VII made alliance with Francis I, thus prevented Charles from attacking the Lutherans and Turks
1534	Suleiman's eastern campaign, took Bagdad, sacked Tabriz. Act of Supremacy, English Reformation. Henry VIII of England excommunicated due to marriage to Ann Boleyn, thus England's break with Rome
1534–50	Pope Paul III
1538	Treaty of Grosswardein, February. Zapolya and Ferdinand signed. In return for Hapsburg protection against Turkish attack, the Hungarian agreed to recognize Ferdinand as his successor. This agreement precipitated a major Turkish attack on Muldavia which started in the late spring.
1540	Death of Zapolya, Suleiman's vassal in Hungary. Suleiman invaded and proclaimed Hungary an Ottoman province—which remained so for nearly a century and a half
1541	Turks seize Buda and threaten Austria. Charles calls on Lutherans for help. Turkish attack reached its height in August 1541. France, Turkey, Cleves, Sweden, Denmark, Scotland made up the Anti-Imperialist League. The Turks returned to Constantinople in September without attempting a direct attack against the Empire or Ferdinand's forces west of Buda
1544	Peace of Crespy: Charles concluded peace with Francis

DATE	EVENT
1545	Council of Trent (March). Charles and Ferdinand sent representatives to Constantinople to seek a truce with the Porte on the basis of *uti possedetis*. Suleiman, anxious to resume his war against Tahmasp, welcomed the Hapsburg terms.
1546	Luther's death, February 18 at Eisleben
1550–55	Pope Julius III
1551	Tripoli falls to Turks
1552	Treaty of Passau: the leaders of a victorious Protestant conspiracy against Charles obtained *de facto* recognition for their religion by this treaty
1555	Peace of Augsburg: On September 25, the Religious Peace of Augsburg formally recorded the decision of the Reichstag by which Lutheranism was recognized as an official religion in Germany and legal equality granted to all worshipers of the faith. Sultan of Turkey sent Devlil Girai Khan, the Krim (Crimea) Khan north. The road to Moscow was unprotected. When he reached there, a fire broke out and in six hours leveled the city, except the Kremlin, within a compass of thirty miles. The Krim Khan, satisfied withdrew without attacking the Kremlin
1555–59	Pope Paul IV
1556	Charles V abdicates, succeeded by Philip II (-1598), during which time Hapsburg power reached its zenith. He was recognized by Paul IV as the "strongest pillar of Catholicism." His wife died after birth of Don Carlos. He married Queen Mary of England in 1554 who died childless in 1558. Crowned king of Spain 1556
1566	Suleiman reached zenith of his reign. Bagdad, Azerbaijan, Tunisia, Tripolitania added. Janissaries spread terror. Hungary, Transylvania, Bessarabia to Vienna in 1529, where he was again defeated. Slow and steady process of decline continued till the twentieth century.

DATE	EVENT

DISMEMBERMENT OF MUSLIM WORLD

Date	Event
1699	Began with Transylvania, Hungary, Austria
1707	Aurangzeb (Akbar's grandson) added whole of India, remained until last sultan was dethroned by British in 1858
1774	Azov to Russia
1783	Crimea
1812	Bessarabia, vast territories in Central Asia. Today Russian Soviets include the free Muslim republics of Azerbaijan, Kazakhstan, Uzbekistan, Turkmenistan, Tadzhikistan, Kughizia
1830	Greece regains independence
1878	Bosnia to Austria. Rumania, Bulgaria, Serbia, Montenegro
1912	Balkan War ended Ottoman suzerainty
1919	Turkey
1921	Jordan
1922	Iraq, Egypt (monarchy)
1926	Lebanon
1936	Egypt independence, republic in 1953
1946	Syria
1947	Pakistan
1949	Indonesia

SOURCES:

Encyclopaedia Britannica, 13th ed., Vol. 17.

Encyclopaedia Britannica, 1971 ed., Vol. 2.

Grousset, Rene. *Conqueror of the World,* Trans. by Marian McKellar and Denis Sinor. New York: The Orion Press. 1966.

Hitti, Philip K. *History of the Arabs,* Second Edition, Revised. London: MacMillan and Co. Ltd. 1940.

Lamb, Harold. *Tamerlane, the Earth Shaker.* Garden City: Garden City Publishing Co. 1928.

Phillips, E. D. *The Mongols.* London: Thames and Hudson. 1969.

Stavrianos, L. S. *The Balkans Since 1453.* New York: Holt, Rinehart and Winston. 1965.

Appendix C
Table of Mohammed's Genealogy

The Tribe of Koreish
(descended from Ishmael, number 96, Appendix A)

GHALIB
. LOWAI
. . ADA (from whom, by descent, OMAR, second caliph)
. . KAAB
. . . MORRAH
. . . . KILAB
. . . . . KUSSAI
. . . . . . ABD MENAF
. . . . AL MUTTALIT
. . . . HASHIM
. . . . ABD UL MUTTALIB
. . . . HARITH
. . . . ZOBEIR
. . . . ABU TALIB
. . . . ALI (who married Fatima, Mohammed's daughter; also fourth caliph and first of Twelvers)
. . . . HASSAN, A.D. 669, Twelver No. 2.
. . . . HUSAYN, A.D. 680. No. 3.
. . . . ALI ZAYN AL ABIDIN, 712, 4.
. . . . MUHAMMAD AL BAQIR, 731, 5.
. . . . JA'FAR AL SADIQ, 765, 6.
. . . . MUSA AL KAZIM, 799, 7.

. . . . ALI AL RIDA, 818, 8.
. . . . MUHAMMAD AL JAWAD,
835, 9.
. . . . ALI AL HADI, 868, 10.
. . . . HASSAN AL ASKARI,
874, 11.
. . . . MUHAMMAD AL
MUNTAZAR (Al Mahdi),
878, 12.
. . . . ZAINAB
. . . . MUHSIN
. . . . ABU LAHIB
. . . . ABDULLAH
. . . . *MOHAMMED*
. . . . FATIMA (and five other children with
Khadijah)
. . . . IBRAHIM (By Mary the Coptic slave. All
except Fatima died before Mohammed and
without issue)
. . . . ABBAS
. . . . HAMZA
. . . . ABD SHEMS
. . . . NAUFAL
. . . . WARAQA (first convert to Christianity)
. . . . ZOHRA (from whom Mohammed's mother, Amina)
. . . . . AMINA (Mohammed's mother)
. . . . TAYM (from whom, by descent, Abu Bakr, first caliph)
. . . . YOKDAY (from whom Khalid)

SOURCES:

Hitti, Philip K. *History of the Arabs,* Second Edition, Revised.
London: MacMillan and Co., Limited. 1940.
Zwemer, Samuel M. *Islam, A Challenge to Faith,* Second Revised
Edition. New York: Student Volunteer Movement for Foreign
Missions. 1909.

Bibliography

1. Ali, Abdullah Yusuf, Trans. *The Holy Koran*, Vols. I and II. New York. Hafner Publishing Company. 1938.
2. Augustine. *Reply to Faustus the Manichaean*, XX. 4, trans. in *BPBF*, 1st series.
3. Barker, Ernest. "The Crusades" in *The Legacy of Islam*, Ed. Sir Thomas Arnold. Oxford: Clarendon Press.
4. Bell, Richard. *The Origin of Islam in its Christian Environment*. The Gunning Lectures. Edinburgh University: Frank Cass & Co., Ltd. 1968.
5. Bethmann, Erich W. *Bridge to Islam*. Nashville, Tenn.: Southern Publishing Association. 1950.
6. Boak, Arthur Edward Romilly. *A History of Rome to 565* A.D., 4th Ed. New York: Macmillan. 1955.
7. Breasted, James Henry. *Development of Religion and Thought in Ancient Egypt*. Introduction by John A. Wilson. Harper Torchbook. New York: Harper and Row. 1959.
8. Bukhari, al-. *Sahih ul-Bukhari*. Arabic Ed. *Mishkat ul-Masabih*.
9. Cumont, Franz. *Oriental Religions in Roman Paganism*. Chicago: The Open Court Pub. Co. 1911.
10. Draper, John William. *History of the Intellectual Development of Europe*. Rev. Ed., Vol. I. New York: Harper and Brothers. 1898.
11. Durant, William James. *The Age of Faith*. A history of medieval civilization—Christian, Islamic, and Judaic—from Constantine to Dante, A.D. 325-1300. New York: Simon Schuster. 1950.
12. Farag, Wadie. "Eschatological Teachings of Islam." M.A. Thesis. Seventh-day Adventist Theological Seminary, 1949.
13. Farnell, Lewis Richard. *The Attributes of God*. The Gifford

Lectures. Delivered at the U. of St. Andrews in the year 1924-1925. Oxford: Clarendon Press. 1925.

14. Fazl, Ahmad. *Mohammed, the Prophet of Islam.*

15. Fischer-Galati, Stephen A. *Ottoman Imperialism and German Protestantism,* 1521-1555. Harvard Historical Monographs XLIII. N. Y.: Octagon. 1972.

16. Frye, Richard N. *The Heritage of Persia.* Cleveland: World Publishing Co. 1963.

17. Gibb, H. A. R. "Literature" in *The Legacy of Islam.* Ed. Sir Thomas Arnold. Oxford: Clarendon Press. 1931.

18. Gibbon, Edward. *The History of the Decline and Fall of the Roman Empire.* Ed. by J. B. Bury. London: Methuen and Co. 1897.

19. Goldziher, Ignaz. *Mohammed and Islam.* New Haven: Yale University Press. 1917.

20. Grimm, Harold J. *The Reformation Era 1500-1650.* New York: The Macmillan Company. 1954.

21. Guillaume, Alfred, Co-editor with Sir Thomas Arnold, *The Legacy of Islam.* Oxford: Clarendon Press. 1931.

22. Harnack, Adolph von. *History of Dogma.* Trans. by Neil Buchanan from 3rd German ed., Vol. IV. New York: Roberts Brothers. 1899.

23. _____. *What Is Christianity?* Trans. Thomas Bailey Saunders. New York: G. P. Putnam's Sons. 1968.

24. Hitti, Philip K. *The Arabs, A Short History.* 5th Ed. New York: St. Martin's Press. 1968.

25. _____. *History of the Arabs.* 2nd Ed. Rev. London: Macmillan and Co. Limited. 1940.

26. Hughes, Thomas Patrick. *A Dictionary of Islam.* Being a Cyclopaedia of the Doctrines, Rites, Ceremonies, and Customs, Together with the Technical and Theological Terms, of the Muhammadan Religion. London: W. H. Allen & Co. 1885.

27. Hyde, Walter Woodburn. *Paganism to Christianity in the Roman Empire.* Philadelphia: University of Pennsylvania Press. 1946.

28. Inamullah, Khan. *God and Man in Contemporary Islamic*

Thought. Proceedings of the Philosophy Symposium held at the American University of Beirut, February 6-10, 1967. Edited with an Introduction by Charles Malik. Beirut: American University of Beirut Centennial Publication. 1972.

29. Kirk, George E. *A Short History of the Middle East From the Rise of Islam to Modern Times.* 7th Rev. Ed. New York: Frederick A. Praeger. 1964.

30. Laing, Gordon J. *Survival of Roman Religion.* New York: Longmans, Green & Co. 1931.

31. Leclerc, L. *Histoire de la medecine arabe.* Paris. 1876.

32. Lot, Ferdinand. *The End of the Ancient World.* Trans. by Philip Leon and Mariette Leon. New York: A. A. Knopf. 1931.

33. Meyerhof, Max. "Science and Medicine" in *The Legacy of Islam.* Ed. Sir Thomas Arnold. Oxford: Clarendon Press. 1931.

34. Moon, James S. and Ian H. Douglas. *Introduction to Islam.* Lucknow, U. P., India: Henry Martyn Institute.

35. Payne, Robert. *The Holy Sword.* New York: Harper and Row. 1959.

36. Phillips, E. D. *The Mongols.* London: Thames and Hudson. 1969.

37. Pickthall, Mohammed Marmaduke. *The Meaning of the Glorious Koran.* An Explanatory Translation. A Mentor Religious Classic. New York: The New American Library. 1953.

38. Pourhadi, Abraham R. "Present Iranian Religious Philosophy and its Relation to Christianity." M.A. Thesis, Seventh-day Adventist Theological Seminary, 1951.

39. Rahman, Fazlur. *Islam.* Garden City: Doubleday & Co. Inc. 1968.

40. Schuon, Frithjof. *Dimensions of Islam.* Trans. by P. N. Townsend. London: George Allen and Unwin Ltd. 1969.

41. Stavrianos, L. S. *The Balkans Since 1453.* New York: Holt, Rinehart and Winston. 1965.

42. Toynbee, Arnold. *Civilization on Trial.* New York: Oxford University Press. 1948.

43. Vaughan, C. D. *Europe and the Turk: A Pattern of Alliances 1350-1700*. Liverpool. 1954.
44. Val, Merry del. "General Rules From the Codes of Canon Law" in *Index of Prohibited Books*. Revised and published by order of His Holiness Pope Pius XI. New ed.; Vatican City: Vatican Polyglot Press. 1930.
45. Waterhouse, Douglas. "Daniel and His Time (623 to 535-33 B.C.)." Unpublished manuscript. Andrews University, Berrien Springs, Mich., 1975.
46. White, Ellen G. *Education*. Mountain View, Calif.: Pacific Press Publishing Association. 1952.
47. _____. *The Great Controversy*. Mountain View, Calif.: Pacific Press Publishing Association. 1950.
48. _____. *The Story of Patriarchs and Prophets*. Mountain View, Calif.: Pacific Press Publishing Association. 1913.
49. _____. *Signs of the Times*. Mountain View, Calif.: Pacific Press Publishing Asociation.
50. Yamani, Sheikh Ahmed Zaki. *God and Man in Contemporary Islamic Thought*. Proceedings of the Philosophy Symposium held at the American University of Beirut, February 6-10, 1967. Edited with an Introduction by Charles Malik. Beirut: American University of Beirut Centennial Publication. 1972.

Dictionaries and Encyclopedias

51. *Encyclopaedia Britannica,* 1971 Ed. London: William Benton. 1971.
52. *Encyclopaedia Britannica,* 13th Ed., Vol. 17. London. 1926.
53. *Seventh-day Adventist Commentary.* Francis D. Nichol, Ed., 10 Volumes. Washington, D. C.: Review and Herald, Pub. Assn. 1958.

Index